Contents

Contents

Section III: Brain-Based Leadership Competencies

Section IV: Going Forward

Acknowledgments

This book would not have been possible without the influence of many special people.

First of all, the unending support my wife, Sherryl, has given me has helped me persevere when the words simply wouldn't come. My three children, Heather, Josh, and Tiffany, have made my life and writing much richer. Tiffany has especially influenced this book as our family has journeyed together with her through almost three decades of fighting the effects of her brain tumor.

Tiffany's neurologist at Rush Medical Center in Chicago, Dr. Marvin Rossi, not only has provided superb medical care for Tiffany but also has inspired me to delve deeper into my journey to understand the brain. Tiffany's good health today is a living example of both God's power and good stewardship of God's gift to us of wise neuroscience practitioners.

My initial editor, Dr. Kathy Armistead, and my editor who finished out the project, Constance Stella, both encouraged me with their excitement about this work and their wise direction to help craft the book into its finished product. Special thanks also to Kelsey Spinnato, my production editor, who skillfully guided me through the final editing and production process.

The neuroscientists at the NeuroLeadership Institute have taught me well through my executive master's degree in the neuroscience of leadership. Special thanks goes to Dr. Golnaz Tabibnia, my primary professor, and Dr. Grace Y. Chang, who edited the book for scientific accuracy.

Special thanks goes to Dr. David Rock, founder of the NeuroLeadership Institute, whose writings first introduced me to how the brain impacts life and leadership. The work at the NeuroLeadership Institute has spurred my passion to learn more about the brain, God's gift to us.

Acknowledgments

My agent, Steve Laube, has consistently guided me through my writing career with his sage advice. This being my fourth book, he has helped me navigate the challenges of writing and publishing.

I must include the gracious people in London, Ontario, at the church where I pastor, West Park Church. They have allowed me to weave brain insight into my teaching and my leadership.

And, finally, I want to thank my savior, Jesus, who paid the ultimate price for me through his sacrificial work on the cross.

About the Author

D r. Charles Stone has been a senior pastor, a teaching pastor, an associate pastor, and a church planter in his thirty-four years of ministry in the United States and Canada. He currently serves as lead pastor at West Park Church in London, Ontario. The most recent of his four earned degrees is an executive master's in the neuroscience of leadership. He feels called to bring into the church a conversation about the brain's impact on life, leadership, and ministry. He regularly blogs about leadership at his website, which is www.charlesstone.com.

Why You Might Want to Read This Book

Now, Therefore, I, George Bush, President of the United States of America, do hereby proclaim the decade beginning January 1, 1990, as the Decade of the Brain. I call upon all public officials and the people of the United States to observe that decade with appropriate programs, ceremonies, and activities.
In Witness Whereof, I have hereunto set my hand this seventeenth day of July, in the year of our Lord nineteen hundred and ninety, and of the Independence of the United States of America the two hundred fifteenth.

—George H. W. Bush

This presidential proclamation began an explosion into brain research. The *decade of the brain* has segued into what looks now to be the *century of the brain*. Since that proclamation from the White House, governments, academia, and businesses have invested billions of research dollars to understand this 3.5-pound organ called the brain. And in February 2013, President Obama proposed a $3 billion project called the BRAIN Initiative to map the human brain, similar to the genome project that mapped our DNA. With the discovery in the early nineties that scientists could actually see what neighborhoods of the brain light up in response to challenges or tasks, functional magnetic resonance imaging (fMRI) has opened up new vistas into how our brains work.

Much of the interest in the brain has been driven by trying to find cures for such brain disorders as Alzheimer's, autism, epilepsy, stroke, mental illness, and Parkinson's, which cost hundreds of billions of dollars each year in medical care and lost work time. And the aging population will continue to fuel research. Interest in the brain has even spawned a new branch of science called *cognitive social neuroscience*, a term popularized in 2000 by two well-respected neuroscientists, Matthew Lieberman and Kevin Ochsner. This field examines how brain functions affect relationships, productivity, emotions, our social lives, and a host of other areas. Entire research labs now focus on this field.

Books about the brain, both scholarly and nonscholarly, fill bookstores today. Many have become best sellers. These books tell us that the keys to health, marketing, happiness, positive emotions, effective parenting, and enduring relationships lie in the brain. Buddhism and other Eastern practices underlie many of these books. Many are written from a nontheistic viewpoint. That is, the authors believe that our essence is simply the sum of brain cell firings (neurons) and hormonal secretions. No more, no less. When brain activity ceases, they believe we cease to exist.

As a result, many Christians view brain science with a wary eye. Some dismiss out of hand what neuroscience can teach us, since they believe those scientists don't believe in God, sound new age–ish, or practice Buddhist meditation. However, most neuroscientists, whatever their views about God, are producing sound research that can complement a Christian's convictions. Most of us hold in common our mutual quest for truth. And as an old preacher once said, "All truth is God's truth."

Dr. John Polkinghorne, an Anglican priest who is a former professor of mathematical physics at Cambridge University and was president of Queens' College, Cambridge, captures this thought with these words: "Science and theology have things to say to each other, since both are concerned with the search for truth attained through motivated belief" (Polkinghorne, 2007).

And Mark Noll, world-renowned Christian historian at Notre Dame named by *Time* magazine in 2005 as one of the twenty-five most influential evangelicals in America, wrote these words about a Christian's motivation to learn about God's creation:

> Coming to know Christ provides the most basic possible motive for pursuing the tasks of human learning. . . . If what we claim about Jesus Christ is true, then evangelicals should be among the most active, most serious, and most open minded advocates of general human learning. Evangelical hesita-

tion about scholarship in general or about pursuing learning wholeheartedly is, in other words, antithetical to the Christ-centered basis of evangelical faith. (Noll, 2011, Kindle e-book loc. 21)

Although I've earned a master's and a doctorate in Christian ministry in addition to my engineering degree, I never heard a seminary professor talk about how the brain impacts leadership, relationships, or preaching and teaching. The unspoken message has been, "You work with the spiritual stuff. Leave the medical and psychological stuff to the doctors, researchers, and counselors." My painful journey that gave me my passion to understand the brain (chapter 2) has led me to resist that unspoken message. As I've incorporated brain insights into my leadership and spiritual life, I've experienced new personal freedom, leadership consistency, and spiritual depth. And brain insight has also helped my teaching and preaching connect to others in a much deeper and lasting way. I believe brain insight can make you a better leader as well.

So, why another book on leadership? With over sixty thousand books on the subject and most workers preferring a better boss to a pay raise (Giang, 2012), apparently we've still got a ways to go to improve how we lead. Many leadership practices were developed in the past to guide leaders to help workers who used their motor skills to make things with their hands (Kluger & DeNisi, 1996). While that's certainly important, much of today's workforce (including pastors and church volunteers) work less with their hands and more with their minds. We need a book for Christian leaders that incorporates what we're learning about brain functioning. It can change the way you lead, lessen your stress, strengthen commitment, and improve team collaboration in your ministry.

I've targeted this book to those who consider themselves leaders and Christians and want to be better at both. You might be a pastor, an associate pastor, a teacher, a trainer, a consultant, a board member, a volunteer leader in your church, or even a business owner or manager. If you lead in any way and want to learn to lead better from a fresh perspective about leadership, this book is for you.

In my growth journey as a pastor-leader, sometimes I've gotten frustrated with how a conversation went with my family, how a leadership meeting went, or how I responded to a critic. I truly wanted those encounters to go well. For some reason, however, something in my head influenced me to say something unhelpful, get emotional, or react. But, I couldn't put my finger on what prompted that behavior. I didn't have the words to describe these internal processes that affected my behavior.

I've since learned that deeply embedded habits and thought patterns actually move further away from the language centers in our brains, which makes it difficult to articulate them or determine what cued them (Duhigg, 2012a). For example, although in the past I've felt my anxiety often rise in board meetings, I couldn't seem to find the words to explain why. However, brain insight has helped me more consistently put my feelings and thoughts into words. As a result, I've been able to manage that anxiety in a board meeting and listen more intently to others.

That's what *Brain-Savvy Leaders* is meant to do. By intersecting biblical insight with insights about the brain, we can develop new learnings and language to help us become better leaders, like actually listening to a board member disagree with you rather than becoming defensive and cutting him or her off.

David Rock, one of today's most prominent voices advocating intersecting neuroscience and leadership, coined the term *neuroleadership*. He's written several books and founded the NeuroLeadership Institute. The website defines neuroleadership in this way: "Neuroleadership is an emerging field of study connecting neuroscientific knowledge with the fields of leadership development, management training, change management, consulting and coaching" (NeuroLeadership Institute, 2013).

That definition brings me to the essence of this book: knowledge gleaned from neuroscience and applied to the art of Christian leadership. In this book, you'll find practical insights that sync with scripture that you can apply in your ministry in these four core leadership domains, two in the personal area and two in the organizational area. This book will show you how to

keep your emotions in check: **emotional regulation**

do your best with what you have: **personal productivity**

foster high-performing teams: **team collaboration**

motivate others to embrace change that lasts: **change management**

The end result fosters significant ministry, effective organizations, and churches that are resilient, cohesive, and outwardly focused. As an example of how brain insight has improved my leadership, I recall in my early ministry days that I'd try to force change in the churches where I served. Often I only made people mad and achieved few lasting results. However, as I've applied brain insight to change management, those who resist change have become more open to it and the change initiatives have become more successful.

The following diagram pictures the four domains you'll learn about. You'll notice a word beneath each domain. Each word refers to an acronym and a related image that I use to outline how to apply each domain to your leadership and ministry. You'll see this diagram often in the book because visuals help us retain and recall information more easily.

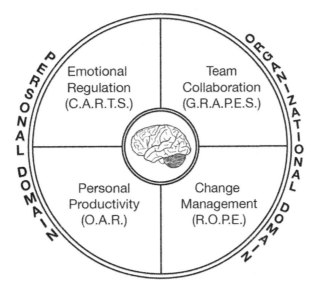

But first, are the Bible and brain science uneasy bedfellows? I address concerns about mixing the two in the chapter that follows.

Section I

Why the Brain and the Bible?

Chapter 1

Brain Science and the Bible: Uneasy Bedfellows?

Brain Surprise 1: *Gratefulness is actually good for brain and body health (see the end of the chapter for the brain basis behind this brain surprise).*

I assume you're reading this book because at some level you see value in understanding how your brain works. You want to lead at your best and hope a book like this will provide tools for your leadership toolbox. Perhaps you're reading it because the brain interests you. Perhaps you're reading this because your ministry or business needs a boost. Whatever your motivation, I believe it's important to address some concerns that intersecting neuroscience with the Bible may raise in some leaders' minds.

My interest lies somewhat in that I'm a geek and enjoy having my mind stretched. I also like technology and gadgets; perhaps you're like that too. I'd buy the latest Apple anything were it not for my wife (and my checking account). Catecholamines, action potentials, and neuroplasticity interest me. Perhaps you're also like me in that you like to "cut to the chase" without a lot of jargon. So I promise to keep the overly technical language to a minimum. If you'd like to read more about the science, you can read the studies listed at the end of the book. I've backed up the book with over two hundred references to scientific articles and research studies.

It's also important to know that I'm not a neuroscientist. I am a pastor-leader who loves to learn. I followed my undergraduate degree in engineering with master of divinity and doctor of ministry degrees. At the publication of this book, I've just completed an executive master's in the neuroscience of leadership. But even with my extensive education, I recognize my limitations writing about neuroscience. So, I hired a highly qualified neuroscientist to review this book.

Dr. Grace Y. Chang (PhD, UCLA) is researcher for the UCLA Center for Research, Evaluation, Standards, and Student Testing and lead professor at the NeuroLeadership Institute. Yet, even with the latest research, I realize that as scientists continue to research the brain, it's highly possible that some facts and studies to which I refer may have been supplanted by new learning since the book was published.

Throughout history great minds have often intersected the study of God's creation with study of the scriptures. That list includes some of these famous people:

- Saint Thomas Aquinas: noted for his work regarding Aristotle and formulation of natural law

- Francis Bacon: considered to be the founder of the scientific method

- René Descartes: key thinker of the Scientific Revolution

- Blaise Pascal: a genius in physics, math, and theology

- Isaac Newton: considered one of the greatest scientists and mathematicians in history

- Louis Pasteur: solved the mystery of rabies and anthrax and developed the first vaccines

- Max Planck: founded quantum mechanics and believed that both religion and science required a belief in God

- Francis Collins: former director of the National Human Genome Research Institute who led it to unravel the human genome

- Brian Kobika: winner of the Nobel Prize in Chemistry in 2012

- Jennifer Wiseman: chief of the laboratory for Exoplanets and Stellar Astrophysics at NASA Goddard Space Flight Center

- Albert Einstein: although not a Christian, he once remarked as a young scientist, "I want to know how God created this world, I am not interested in this or that phenomenon, in the spectrum of this or that element. I want to know His thoughts, the rest are details." One of his famous sayings was, "Science without religion is lame, religion without science is blind" *(Famous scientists,* 2011).

These brilliant Christian scientists point to this reality: God gave us a brain not just because our body needed a command and control center to direct it but because God enjoys seeing us steward our brains for his glory. God relishes young minds (and old) peering into microscopes, hooking electronic parts together in garages to create computers, and going to schools of higher learning to become great scientists, engineers, pastors, and poets. From a neuroscience perspective, it's interesting to note that a Christian in the 1600s, British doctor Thomas Willis, pioneered research into the brain and even coined the term "neurology."

The scriptures often refer to concepts about the brain, the soul, and the mind. Although the Bible doesn't use the word *brain* and says nothing about neuronal activity, the word *mind(s)* is used over 160 times. As one author wrote, the biblical writers often used the words *heart, bowels,* and *kidneys* to describe the seat of our emotions and volition. "According to the Bible, the heart is the seat of will, the kidneys are the seat of motivation and the bowels the seat of emotions" (Gijsbers, 2003). Interestingly, neuroscientists have discovered that one part of our brains, called the insula, actually receives information from our visceral organs (heart, intestines, sex organs) and gives us that "gut feeling" about some things and also plays a large role in our emotions and intuition. Some have even called our visceral organs our "second brain" (Hadhazy, 2010).

In the Old Testament when the names of body parts were used literally, they were usually limited to the internal organs of sacrificial animals (Steinberg, 2003). However, words like *heart* or *kidneys* were almost always used metaphorically. We often use those words in the same way. When we say someone broke our heart, we mean metaphorically that he or she emotionally hurt us, not that our heart physically broke. Even though our emotions largely originate in our brains, we don't use an anatomically correct phrase like, "Her actions caused my subcortical limbic system to secrete neurotransmitters and hormones that dampened my prefrontal cortex's thinking ability and activated my sympathetic nervous system, which increased my heart rate and respiration."

Heart in the Old Testament could mean the inner person, intellect, memory, emotions, desire, will, and courage, all functions of the brain. When God hardened Pharaoh's heart, it could have meant that God kept Pharaoh from using his mind to think clearly enough to avoid the pending disaster that awaited Egypt.

The New Testament uses the words for *mind, spirit,* and *soul* in a similar way, but the word for *mind* (*nous*) takes a more prominent role than in the Old Testament. Consider how pervasive the concept for mind is in the New Testament.

- What goes on in our minds can cause us to stumble.
    o "But he turned to Peter and said, 'Get behind me, Satan. You are a stone that could make me stumble, for you are not thinking God's thoughts but human thoughts.'" (Matt 16:23)

- We're to love God with our minds.
    o "He replied, 'You must love the Lord your God with all your heart, with all your being, and with all your mind.'" (Matt 22:37)

- Repeated sin can warp our minds and further inappropriate behavior.
    o "Since they didn't think it was worthwhile to acknowledge God, God abandoned them to a defective mind to do inappropriate things." (Rom 1:28)

- Our spiritual battle largely occurs in our minds.
    o "But I see a different law at work in my body. It wages a war against the law of my mind and takes me prisoner with the law of sin that is in my body." (Rom 7:23)

- Our minds direct where we place our spiritual focus.
  - "People whose lives are based on selfishness think about selfish things, but people whose lives are based on the Spirit think about things that are related to the Spirit. The attitude that comes from selfishness leads to death, but the attitude that comes from the Spirit leads to life and peace. So the attitude that comes from selfishness is hostile to God. It doesn't submit to God's Law, because it can't." (Rom 8:5-7)
- Scripture prioritizes changing our minds to think God's thoughts.
  - "Don't be conformed to the patterns of this world, but be transformed by the renewing of your minds so that you can figure out what God's will is—what is good and pleasing and mature." (Rom 12:2)
- Our minds are finite in what they can understand.
  - "But this is precisely what is written: God has prepared things for those who love him that no eye has seen, or ear has heard, or that haven't crossed the mind of any human being." (1 Cor 2:9)
- The believer's mind has been mysteriously endowed with the mind of Christ.
  - "Who has known the mind of the Lord, who will advise him? But we have the mind of Christ." (1 Cor 2:16)
- Spirituality engages the mind.
  - "If I pray in a tongue, my spirit prays but my mind isn't productive. What should I do? I'll pray in the Spirit, but I'll pray with my mind too; I'll sing a psalm in the Spirit, but I'll sing the psalm with my mind too." (1 Cor 14:14-15)
- Satan can blind the eyes of unbelievers to keep them from understanding Jesus.
  - "The god of this age has blinded the minds of those who don't have faith so they couldn't see the light of the gospel that reveals Christ's glory. Christ is the image of God." (2 Cor 4:4)
- We're to focus our minds' attention on certain things, and

attention is a core component of learning. In other words, thinking affects behavior.

> o "Think about the things above and not things on earth." (Col 3:2)
>
> o "From now on, brothers and sisters, if anything is excellent and if anything is admirable, focus your thoughts on these things: all that is true, all that is holy, all that is just, all that is pure, all that is lovely, and all that is worthy of praise." (Phil 4:8)

- Self-control is a component of mental activity.

> o "Therefore, once you have your minds ready for action and you are thinking clearly..." (1 Pet 1:13)

- Lack of faith negatively impacts the mind.

> o "Whoever asks shouldn't hesitate. They should ask in faith, without doubting. Whoever doubts is like the surf of the sea, tossed and turned by the wind. People like that should never imagine that they will receive anything from the Lord. They are double-minded, unstable in all their ways." (Jas 1:9)

With this scriptural backdrop that I believe supports intersecting spiritual leadership with brain insight, I quote a leading neuroscientist, Andrew B. Newberg, who studies and writes about neurotheology, how theology and neuroscience integrate. Although he does not profess to be a Christian, he represents a growing number of neuroscientists who appreciate faith perspectives into how the mind works:

> The ability to relate theological concepts to mental and brain processes does not mean in any way to imply that these concepts have been reduced to brain chemistry, but rather they may provide at the very least, a new perspective, and at most, an important method for further evaluating the true basis of those concepts. (Newberg, 2010, Kindle e-book loc. 95)

In other words, spirituality cannot be reduced to brain chemicals and firing of neurons. And even as scientists debate if the mind and the brain are the same things, there seems to exist a clear interplay between our brains/minds and our spiritual lives and leadership.

Newberg also writes, "Neurotheology should be prepared to take full advantage of the advances in fields of science such as functional brain imaging, cognitive neuroscience, psychology, and genetics. On the other hand, neurotheological scholarship should also be prepared to engage the full range of theological issues" (Newberg, 2010, Kindle e-book loc. 280).

So in summary, these beliefs have guided my thoughts in this book. I believe we were created in God's image and that our souls are more than our brains. Because of sin, we were separated from God. God saw our predicament and made a way for that relationship to be restored. It came through the person of Jesus Christ, who experienced the virgin birth as God's Son, lived a sinless life, died a sacrificial death on a cross for our sins, rose from the dead, and lives today in heaven. One day Jesus will return and restore everything back to its intended purpose.

Anyone can come into a relationship with God through repentance and faith in Jesus's finished work on the cross. God's spirit changes us to become more like God in belief and behavior through a process called sanctification, but only as we choose to cooperate with him. Through the process of sanctification, God changes not only how we think and behave but also our brain structure. Our bodies and brains embody our souls, of which one component is our minds. We have a free will, and by exercising that free will, we can actually change the wiring in our brains, a process called neuroplasticity.

Scripture promises that when believers die, although the neurons in their brains no longer fire, their souls go to be with the Lord as they await a brand-new body at the great resurrection. After that they will live forever in heaven to enjoy God's presence and the fellowship of other believers. As a Christian, this is my hope. But in the meantime, I want to make the most of my days on earth as a follower of Jesus and as a Christian leader. Yet, in my case, God has used personal pain to whet my interest in the brain. In the next chapter I briefly write about that journey.

A brief note to the reader: The first page of each chapter begins with an interesting neuroscience insight I call a *brain surprise*. At the end of each chapter you will find a short explanation with source material about the neuroscience behind the brain surprise.

The science behind . . . *Brain Surprise 1*: *Gratefulness is actually good for brain and body health* (Korb, 2012).

In one study researchers asked participants to keep a daily journal of what they were grateful for. They asked another group to write about what annoyed them. The group who recorded what they were grateful for showed greater determination, attention, enthusiasm, and energy compared to the other group. In another study the same researchers discovered that even keeping a weekly gratefulness journal reduced aches and pains. And in a Chinese study, gratefulness decreased depression and improved sleep.

Chapter 2

The Agonizing Journey: Brain Science Becomes Personal

Brain Surprise 2: *Your devotional life just might help you live a longer life.*

I squirted a glob of caramel-colored antibiotic soap on my hands and realized that my sink didn't have any faucets. I didn't want to look dumb, so I quickly glanced at the surgeon next to me as he leaned over the other galvanized sink. His sink was missing faucets as well, but as he leaned against the side of the sink, water automatically came out of the goosenecked spigot. I mimicked what he did, and the water flowed in a gentle stream without splashing onto my blue scrubs. I lathered with the bristly sterilized sponge and focused on my fingernails as the nurse had instructed.

As I scrubbed, my thoughts drifted to a nameless father who stood in the exact same place perhaps two hours earlier, as had hundreds of dads before him. A new lease on life, permanent disability, or even death awaited that dad's child. The same possibilities awaited my daughter. My fears would soon turn to faith through the unintended instruction of my five-year-old daughter, and God would begin to birth a new passion into my soul.

Five years earlier I was overwhelmed with joy as I nestled in my arms for the first time my newborn, Tiffany. She was our "surprise" child after having two other children. My wife, Sherryl, had experienced her easiest pregnancy with Tiffany, and we enjoyed a problem-free first year with her, until her first Christmas.

We would often spend Christmas in the small town of Laurel, Mississippi, with Sherryl's family. I would joke with my friends and tell them that the best vacations for me consisted of all-you-can-eat buffets, long naps, and big-screen TV football. Our trips to Mississippi gave me exactly that experience, until that year.

Christmas day arrived with the expected commotion that three excited preschoolers bring. Sherryl's dad had strategically placed the video camera to capture their delighted expressions when they ran into the living room to see the gifts piled under the tree. After we thanked Jesus for his gifts to us, we excitedly watched them tear into the colorful packages. After what seemed like forever, they opened the last one, and we moved into the kitchen for our Christmas breakfast.

The two older kids sat at the table, while I got high-chair duty with Tiffany. As I cajoled Tiffany to eat pureed peaches and scrambled eggs, I noticed something unusual about her right eye. It seemed to quiver like Jell-O. None of our other kids' eyes had done this, and as you might imagine, it was disconcerting. The next day we saw a pediatrician, and he told us not to worry because it was a common condition. He suggested, however that we see a pediatric eye specialist when we got back to our home in Atlanta. When we returned we quickly scheduled the appointment. After that doctor examined her, he too cautioned us not to worry. He scheduled a CT scan just to be sure. A few days later we took her to the hospital for what the doctor described as a routine scan. If anything unusual showed up, he promised to call. This is a picture of what a normal brain scan looks like.

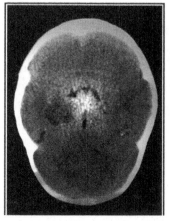

We believed the best and went home trying not to worry. As we walked in the front door, the phone rang, and the words I heard would forever change our lives. This scan is why the doctor called us. This was a scan of Tiffany's one-year-old brain.

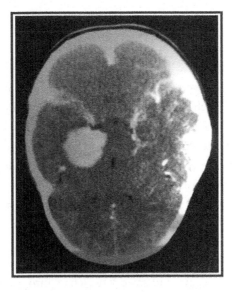

The doctor tried to minimize the weight of the message as best he could. He first commented that the scan showed an irregularity. My mind raced. *What in the world is an irregularity?* As he continued, he said, "The scan revealed a lesion [the big white spot on her scan that we later saw]."

A lesion, I thought. *Could that be a simple problem that antibiotics could treat?*

Then he clarified what he was mustering the courage to tell me. I felt as if someone had kicked me in the stomach when he said, "Your daughter has a brain tumor."

I don't remember how I ended the conversation, nor do I remember how I broke the news to my wife. I do remember, however, weeping uncontrollably as I held our precious daughter in my arms. Life would now take on new meaning as we would fight to save her life. Our saga would continue for the next twenty-five years.

Fast-forward four years. After two brain surgeries by the time she had turned four, multiple doctor's visits, and years of therapy, we found another dangerous brain surgery now facing Tiffany. However, even with the pain she had experienced up to this point, she exuded a faith that far exceeded her years.

In a poignant way, her faith would soon lift ours. In the months before, she had learned her alphabet in her Christian kindergarten by memorizing scripture verses. A Bible verse corresponded to each letter of the alphabet. For example, she learned the verse, "All have sinned and fall short of the glory of God" for the letter *a*, "Believe on the Lord Jesus Christ and you will be saved" for the letter *b*, and so on. Before we left for the hospital I asked Tiffany if she wanted to choose a theme verse for her upcoming surgery. She made her selection and planted the verse in her heart. This verse would soon stir us to a level of faith we had never experienced.

I felt that I had finally scrubbed long enough to kill any germs hidden beneath my fingernails. After I tied my blue scrubs, put on the blue hair net, and wrapped my shoes with blue footies, the nurse helped me with the final piece, the white paper face mask. She said the surgeons were now ready, so I slowly wheeled Tiffany in her kid-sized wheelchair into the operating room. This hospital would allow one parent to take the child into the operating room so that the last image the child would see would be that of a parent. As we entered, it took a few moments for my eyes to adjust to the bright lights. The anesthesiologist pointed to the small metal operating table that glistened in the light. He asked me to lay her there. As I gently placed her on this cold metal platform, I thought about how Abraham must have felt when he placed Isaac on the altar.

As the anesthesiologists began her IV, I suggested that Tiffany tell the doctors the verse she had chosen. They awkwardly listened and mumbled something like, "How sweet." As the anesthesia slowly trickled into her body, our eyes locked for one last moment before her eyes glazed over and rolled back into her head. As she fell asleep, I wondered if I would ever see her alive again.

Our Christian surgeon, who was also world famous, Dr. Ben Carson of Johns Hopkins Hospital, told us that the surgery would last about five hours and that a nurse would give us an hourly update. Heaviness pressed upon our hearts, but we trusted that Tiffany was in good hands.

Five hours later the recovery room nurses wheeled her out on a small gurney and told us to meet them in the intensive care area. As we entered the unit, the frigid temperature caused me to catch my breath, and I squinted as my pupils adjusted to the intense lighting. Even as I write this chapter, I can almost feel the heaviness that I felt then.

A respirator's rhythmic *"cu-cu…cu-cu…cu-cu"* to my right caught my attention, and I glanced into the room. Two bleary-eyed parents gingerly caressed their sick child's hand. My heavy heart became heavier still. I was not prepared to enter the rarefied world of a pediatric intensive care unit.

As we approached the curtained cubicle to our left, we found Tiffany bundled beneath several white hospital blankets. Slightly bloody plastic tubes protruded from her head, nose, and arms. Thick bandages hugged her head. My eyes welled up with tears as she awakened, and our eyes locked again.

Then, in a pained, raspy voice, she whispered the words of her theme verse: "F…Fear not, for I am with thee, Isaiah 43:5."

As Dr. Carson, his two assistants, and my wife and I stood there, we experienced a holy moment. In this place filled with gut-wrenching pain and heartache, the spontaneous words of simple faith from a five-year-old indelibly etched themselves on our hearts. Our faith has never been the same.

I must, however, make one correction before I continue. When she quoted her verse, it was actually the second sentence she spoke. The first thing she said was, "I want a Coke." Through my tears I can still smile at that.

Since that time over twenty years ago, Tiffany has continued to live out her strong faith. She recovered well from that surgery, but her trials were not over.

When she entered puberty and hormones began to surge into her body, she developed horrible symptoms. She experienced nausea and vomiting almost every day. Some days she threw up over a hundred times. I'm not exaggerating. She experienced dizziness, head tremors, and often could not walk without assistance. She couldn't go to school, so teachers would come into our home to teach her. When she'd study, often she'd suddenly forget almost everything she had learned in the previous few days. It seemed as if someone had pushed a "reset" switch in her brain.

We tried to find a solution, thinking that the issue was intestinal. After extensive testing, we ruled that out. While we lived in California, the doctors began to think that something more was happening inside her brain, even though the tumor had stopped growing. They tried medicine that didn't help. She had a vagal nerve stimulator implanted in her chest that sent electrical impulses into her brain at a set frequency via the vagal nerve. They theorized that it would disrupt the electrical misfiring that could be causing her symptoms. It didn't work.

We soon moved to Chicago, and Tiffany spent several days at a time in the epilepsy EEG monitoring wing at three different hospitals. The doctors still couldn't find what caused her problems. They believed she was having seizures but could never capture one. They assumed they were coming from the right side of her head where the surgeons had entered her brain during the previous three surgeries. During one hospital stay, they finally captured a seizure but were shocked that it came from the opposite side. At first the doctor was worried that the assistants had accidentally switched the electrodes to the wrong side. Upon inspection, they confirmed that they had been correctly attached. Since the seizure came from her left side and her right temporal lobe was essentially nonfunctioning due to the surgeries, that doctor said there wasn't much he could do because surgery would not be possible. He said he would try more medications. They didn't help.

We then saw a doctor at Rush University Medical Center, Dr. Marvin Rossi, who became a godsend to us. He took special interest in Tiffany and began to extensively map her brain. She was entered into an experimental study and had a device called a responsive neurostimulator (RNS) implanted into her brain. The neurosurgeons implanted probes deep into the part of her brain where Dr. Rossi believed the seizures originated. The RNS then monitored her brain activity acting as a tiny, real-time EEG device. When it detected a possible seizure, it fired an electrical impulse to stop it.

The RNS clearly helped, but Tiffany still was not out of the woods. After she became one of the most studied brains at Rush, the neurology team suggested that Tiffany undergo a temporal lobectomy, a procedure that would remove the damaged temporal lobe. They theorized that the damaged right temporal lobe kept pinging the good left temporal lobe until it eventually gave in and seized, causing an electrical storm in her brain. They call this brain activity an "action potential," when the brain gets enough neuronal stimulation to finally fire. In Tiffany's case, the firing resulted in a temporal lobe petite mal seizure, one barely recognizable outwardly but causing pervasive and terrible postseizure symptoms for her.

Tiffany responded well to the surgery, even though she required a second surgery two days later to stop brain fluid leakage. Since then, however, we thank God that Tiffany has been seizure-free. She's currently studying to be a hospital chaplain.

———

Through six brain surgeries, multiple hospitalizations, and MEG, SPECT, PET, CT, and MRI scans, my wife and I have walked alongside Tiffany for twenty-five years in the rarefied world of neurologists and neurosurgeons. Through Tiffany's suffering I've seen what happens to the body when the brain doesn't work properly.

As a pastor-leader I've also seen how leaders can hurt other people by what they say and do. I've also let my emotions control and negatively affect my leadership and relationships. I've seen change initiatives fall flat on their faces. I've observed teams not work together well. I've seen sermons simply bomb. As a result I've wondered, aside from actual physical problems with the brain, as in Tiffany's case, could the brain also affect how we lead and communicate in ways we've not considered? Could something about the brain lie behind ineffective leadership that I've seen in myself, even though I believed my heart and motives were right? Was I missing something, perhaps about the brain, that could help me lead better?

I then read a book that began to answer some of my questions: *Your Brain at Work* by Dr. David Rock. I couldn't put it down. I read it three times and bought the audiobook and listened to it three times. The book began to open my eyes to the fact that our brains do impact leadership in multiple domains. Dr. Rock had backed his claims with neuroscience research that suggests that brain processes profoundly impact leadership areas such as decision making, problem solving, emotional regulation, collaboration, and change management. I began to read other books and listen to lectures. I was so intrigued about the application to Christian leadership that I enrolled in a master's program in neuroleadership.

Then I realized that through my experiences with Tiffany and through what I was learning about the brain, God was planting a new passion in my soul: to bring neuroscience into the conversation about and with Christian leaders, so that leaders can have the benefit of the knowledge now available.

I'm convinced that God wants me to champion how brain science can help leaders. I haven't looked back since. This book is a product of that passion.

During the past few years, I've taught well over a thousand leaders nationally and internationally about how to apply brain insight to leadership. The talks always intrigue leaders. They soak up what I teach and want more. I hope this book will stir you to learn more about how understanding this gift from God, the brain, can make you a better leader. Such insight not only can help you lead better but also can help you grow spiritually. That's the topic for another brain-based book I'll write one day.

Neuroscience is like a magnifying glass. Magnifying glasses help us see things that we otherwise could not see. But for a magnifying glass to work, it requires a strong light source. That strong light source is the light from God's word, the Bible, and ultimately Jesus, the light of the world. As Pope Paul VI wrote, "Only in the mystery of the incarnate Word does the mystery of man take on light" (Paul VI, 1965).

And as Mark Noll has written, "The light of Christ illuminates the laboratory, his speech is the fount of communication, he makes possible the study of humans in all their interactions, he is the source of all life, he provides the wherewithal for every achievement of human civilization, he is the telos of all that is beautiful. He is, among many other titles, the Christ of the Academic Road" (Noll, 2011, Kindle e-book loc. 310).

In the next chapter we look at five biblical reasons and six practical benefits of why leaders should become brain savvy. In chapters 4 and 5, I introduce you to the brain's parts and what I call its players, the brain activity in those brain parts that impacts leadership. Although you may be tempted to skip these chapters, I encourage you to read them because the working terminology will help the application chapters make better sense.

In section 3 we'll unpack four key leadership areas to which neuroscience speaks. I've included this diagram again to illustrate the two personal domains and the two organizational domains. The acronyms in the diagram represent key aspects applicable to each domain.

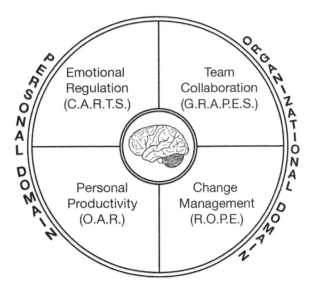

The science behind...*Brain Surprise 2*: *Your devotional life just might help you live longer.*

At the end of our chromosomes lie protective caps called telomeres that are linked to longevity. Apparently, the longer your telomeres, all else being equal, the longer you live. Long-term stress shortens them, and mindfulness (see chapter 5) apparently helps lengthen them. For a Christian, mindfulness practices, such as meditation on scripture and reflective prayer, which we often do in our devotional time, may possibly help us live longer (Epel et al., 2009).

Chapter 3

The Brain-Savvy Leader: Why You Should Become One

Brain Surprise 3: *If you feel drowsy, chewing gum may make you more alert.*

I've never met a good leader who didn't want to improve. We all want to develop our skills and competencies to leverage our gifts for maximum Kingdom impact. When we become more brain savvy, we enhance our ability to make a difference for God in our relationships, our work, and our ministries. And I don't believe neuroleadership (applying neuroscience insight to leadership) is a fad. It's here to stay. However, as applicable and interesting as it may be, we must run it through the lens of scripture. Hopefully chapter 1 provided a sound theological basis for intersecting the brain and the Bible. In this chapter I extend those thoughts with biblical reasons for and practical benefits of becoming a brain-savvy leader.

Biblical Reasons to Become a Brain-Savvy Leader

1. When We Study Our Brains, We Study What Christ Has Made

Scripture makes clear that as part of the Trinity, Jesus helped create the universe. From the beginning, Jesus has been involved. Everything in the universe has Jesus's "thumbprint" upon it.

The Word was with God in the beginning. Everything came into being through the Word, and without the Word nothing came into being. (John 1:2-3)

The Son is the image of the invisible God,

    the one who is first over all creation,

Because all things were created by him:

    both in the heavens and on the earth, the things that are visible and the things that are invisible.

        Whether they are thrones or powers, or rulers or authorities,

all things were created through him and for him. (Col 1:15-16)

In these final days, though, he spoke to us through a Son. God made his Son the heir of everything and created the world through him. (Heb 1:2)

Jesus is not only redeemer but was also creator as well. So studying God's creation (i.e., through neuroscience) should not lead us away from God as some may fear. Certainly, as history has shown, many have misused what we've learned about God's creation. But that possibility should not cause us to shun learning (Noll, 2011, Kindle e-book loc. 338) for "all the treasures of wisdom and knowledge are hidden in him" (Col 2:3). On the contrary, as Noll wrote, "If what we claim about Jesus Christ is true, then evangelicals should be among the most active, most serious, and the most open minded advocates of general human learning" (Noll, 2011, Kindle e-book loc. 23).

In fact, the more I've learned about how our brains and minds work, the more I've experienced the awe of God. Although materialist reduction-ists (those who believe that matter and energy is all there is, that we have no soul, and that no afterlife exists) have written many of today's popular brain books, I've not felt threatened by their underlying philosophies. Rather, I've gained a greater appreciation for the grandeur, creativity, and majesty of our Creator-God. My strongly "encoded" theological basis has guided my think-ing. *Encoding* is the neuroscience term used to describe the amazing process when information that comes into our minds is transformed into beliefs, knowledge, habits, memories, and values. Studying and teaching the Bible for decades has produced huge connected bundles of neurons, or mental highways, built around a Christian worldview that now profoundly influences my life through the way I view the human condition, how I treat others, and what I do with the time and resources God has given me.

2. When We Learn about Our Brains, We Are More Able to Honor and Glorify God

Colossians 1:16 tells us that all things are made "for him." Everything is made for the glory of God—the snow I see outside my window as I write this sentence, the barren tree I see whose silhouette the snow frames, my fingers as I type, and our brains. So if our brains are part of the "all things" God created, it naturally follows that we should use our brains to bring God glory. The more I learn and know about it, the more I can use it for Kingdom purposes.

3. Deeply Embedded Virtues and Values Are Intimately Tied to the Workings of Our Brains, so the More We Know about It, the More We Can Leverage It to Help Make Our Character Stick

We have both a body and a soul mysteriously unified. What goes on in our souls affects our bodies and brains. What we pay attention to can actually change our brains' neuropathways—their *plasticity*. If you regularly read, study, and apply God's word, you will create connections in your brain that reinforce a biblical worldview. Likewise, our body influences our soul. For example, the next time you don't sleep well, you'll find it more difficult to pay attention to God's quiet voice in your devotional time the next day. Sleepy bodies affect our minds and, hence, our effectiveness.

King David understands this body-soul connection. Once, when he refused to confess his sin, he experienced tremendous physical problems: "When I kept quiet, my bones wore out; I was groaning all day long—every day, every night!—because your hand was heavy upon me. My energy was sapped as if in a summer drought" (Ps 32:3-4). He again revisits this in Psalm 38:5-7 when he writes: "My wounds reek; they are all infected because of my stupidity. I am hunched over, completely down; I wander around all day long, sad. My insides are burning up; there's nothing in my body that isn't broken."

The book of Proverbs often links the state of our minds to physical health and wholeness:

- "Trust in the LORD with all your heart; don't rely on your own intelligence. Know him in all your paths, and he will keep your ways straight. Don't consider yourself wise. Fear the LORD and turn away from evil." (Prov 3:5-7)

- "Pleasant words are flowing honey, sweet to the taste and healing to the bones." (Prov 16:24)

- "A peaceful mind gives life to the body, but jealousy rots the bones." (Prov 14:30)

- "A joyful heart helps healing, but a broken spirit dries up the bones." (Prov 17:22)

Long before the days of neuroscience, the mother of John and Charles Wesley, Susanna, understood this amazing connection. She wrote this insight to John on January 8, 1725: "Man is a compound being, a strange mixture of spirit and matter; or, rather, a creature wherein those opposite principles are united without mixture, yet each principle, after an incomprehensible manner, subject to the influence of the other" (Clarke, 1824, pp. 330–31).

4. When We Understand How Our Minds and Brains Work, We Can Help Others More Consistently Grow in Their Walks with Christ

Dr. Donald Hebb (1904–1985) became an expert in his time on how people learn and is considered the father of neuropsychology. He studied how neurons affect learning, resulting in what is commonly called Hebb's law. Essentially he theorized that when neurons consistently "fire together, they wire together." In other words, we learn what we pay attention to because it gets wired into our brains. What we pay attention to creates new pathways and connections in our brains. It's the essence of neuroplasticity, the brain's ability to change. As one neuroscientist has said, our brains are more flexible than we ever thought, more like Play-Doh than porcelain (Ratey, 2013, p. 35).

The Apostle Paul gives us a key verse related to this concept in Romans 12:2:

> Don't be conformed to the patterns of this world, but be transformed by the renewing of your minds so that you can figure out what God's will is—what is good and pleasing and mature.

In Romans 12:1 he transitions from Christianity's theological foundation, chapters 1–11, to the practical implications. He says that a renewal process results in a life conformed to Christ rather than to culture. God changes us to be conformed to what God's will is—*what is good and pleasing and mature*, beliefs and behaviors every Christian should seek. However, Paul links spiritual transformation to an ongoing rather than a discreet process that occurs in our minds, which he calls *renewing of the mind*. The word *renew* comes from the word we use for metamorphosis, beautifully seen when a caterpillar transforms into a butterfly. Paul says that a key to such lasting spiritual change lies in what goes on in our minds, in contrast to many cults in that day that played down rationality. As the Holy Spirit changes our inner being, including our minds, the Holy Spirit creates outward Christlike attitudes that show up in our behavior.

This spiritual transformation will never passively just "happen." Rather, it demands our cooperation with the Holy Spirit, as well as wise leadership and effective teaching from brain-savvy leaders. The processes within our brains and minds profoundly impact spiritual growth. And the more we know about how people learn and how their brains change, the more effective our spiritual growth efforts will become and the greater our capacity for significant ministry. When we apply brain insight, we can design our presentations, sermons, training strategies, classes, and other learning environments to maximize learning and life transformation.

5. *The Key Theological Word* Repentance *Implies That Something Happens in Our Minds When We Repent*

The Greek word for repentance, *metanoia*, means a fundamental change of thinking that results in a change in belief and behavior. Conversion, turning from our sins to Jesus, results in a change toward Christlikeness in all the aspects of our lives, our attitudes, thoughts, and behaviors. Luke wrote: "Produce fruit that shows you have changed your hearts and lives" (Luke 3:8). The process of repentance is necessary for salvation. "You know I have testified to both Jews and Greeks that they must change their hearts and lives as they turn to God and have faith in our Lord Jesus" (Acts 20:21). So with repentance something fundamentally changes in us as we turn from sin as the dominant principle of our lives to new life in Christ. Implicit, then, with coming to faith in Christ is also a mental or neuronal change.

The Bible also uses the word for ongoing repentance in the Christian life, turning from specific sins we commit after salvation.

> Watch yourselves! If your brother or sister sins, warn them to stop. If they change their hearts and lives, forgive them. Even if someone sins against you seven times in one day and returns to you seven times and says, "I am changing my ways," you must forgive that person. (Luke 17:3-4)

> Now I'm glad—not because you were sad but because you were made sad enough to change your hearts and lives. You felt godly sadness so that no one was harmed by us in any way. (2 Cor 7:9)

So a life that experiences continuous growth requires that we regularly confess and repent of our sins. Sanctification, the process of ongoing conformity to the life of Christ, requires an ongoing change in our thinking, which also changes the neural pathways in our brains. Sanctification sculpts new neuronal pathways to align with God's word. Remember Hebb's law, neurons that "fire together, wire together"? The more we pay attention to God's truth, the more our brains change, and thus our thinking changes. So, repentance is both an event and a process, a gift and a response. It is both mental and behavioral change, internal and external. We become more like Jesus in our beliefs and in our behavior.

Joel Green comments on how tangible repentance is: "We discover...that repentance in Luke-Acts will not be a theological abstraction, but aimed at a transformation of day-to-day patterns of thinking, feeling, believing, and behaving" (Green, 2008, p. 123).

When we come to faith, God gives us a new mental framework, his word, through which we now view the world. God changes and is changing us at the deepest level possible, including changing our thinking at a neuronal level as we embrace his thinking more and more (again, recall Hebb's law). What was previously incomprehensible about the life and work of Jesus is now comprehensible through God's spirit as this verse describes:

> After he took his seat at the table with them, he took the bread, blessed and broke it, and gave it to them. Their eyes were opened and they recognized him, but he disappeared from their sight. They said to each other, "Weren't our hearts on fire when he spoke to us along the road and when he explained the scriptures for us?" (Luke 24:30)

Also, an experience in the Apostle Paul's life points to how Jesus gives us new spiritual comprehension when we repent and place our faith in God. When Paul appeared before Herod Agrippa II and Festus and proclaimed Christ, Festus interrupted him with, "You've lost your mind, Paul! Too much learning is driving you mad!" (Acts 26:24-26). Festus could not wrap his mind around the resurrection of Jesus because his spiritual faculty, his spirit, was dead without Christ. He was spiritually blind. One prophecy states that Jesus himself would give sight to the blind (Ps 146:8). While he certainly physically healed the blind, this statement also implies that he gives to anyone who repents what they need to know him personally (the Spirit), which Festus lacked.

The Apostle Paul captures the essence and result of true repentance in these verses:

> So then, from this point on we won't recognize people by human standards. Even though we used to know Christ by human standards, that isn't how we know him now. So then, if anyone is in Christ, that person is part of the new creation. The old things have gone away, and look, new things have arrived! (2 Cor 5:16)

6. Since the Brain Is Part of the Body, We Must Honor God with Our Brains

> Or don't you know that your body is a temple of the Holy Spirit who is in you? Don't you know that you have the Holy Spirit from God, and you don't belong to yourselves? You have been bought and paid for, so honor God with your body. (1 Cor 6:19-20)

This passage applies to the members of the body of Christ. In this passage, Paul is not addressing individuals but the entire group. This means that as our individual brains change, this change will also affect our church as a body of believers as well as us personally. Together we glorify God with our bodies, which include our brains, when we eat right, sleep right, exercise, and do acts of charity and mercy as a group of believers.

Let's move on and consider a few practical benefits.

Practical Benefits of Becoming a Brain-Savvy Leader

Not only do theological reasons undergird why we should learn how our brains work, but also practical ones do as well. When we "get under the hood," so to speak, and understand how our brains shape our beliefs and behavior, we can personally grow and help those around us grow as well. An important term related to the practical side, *social cognitive neuroscience*, is used to describe the field that applies neuroscience to how we behave and relate to others. Neuroleadership, then, focuses on how that science can help leaders lead better.

The average day of a leader includes multiple organizational and individual activities such as these.

- Planning how he or she will spend the time for the day that likely includes a task list longer than what can be accomplished

- Preparing for an important meeting

- Personal growth and development

- Dealing with the frustration he or she feels with an overbearing boss, an underperforming employee, or a church volunteer with a bad attitude

- Meetings with coworkers, clients, parishioners, or supervisors

- Developing teams and individuals, which may include conflict resolution, motivation, coaching, training, or hiring and firing

- Juggling responses to scores if not hundreds of e-mails

How well you perform such tasks will determine your leadership effectiveness. And what happens inside your brain impacts how well you perform them. The better you understand how your brain and the brains of those around you work, the more effectively you can lead. So consider these practical reasons for becoming a brain-savvy leader.

1. You Can Improve How Others Receive Feedback from You

Almost every year in my thirty-five years in ministry leadership, I've spent many hours preparing and delivering multiple staff performance reviews. I was surprised to recently learn that I may have been wasting my time.

In a meta-study (a study of the studies), researchers discovered that only 30 percent of feedback and performance reviews actually help (Kluger & DeNisi, 1996). They discovered that 30 percent have no impact and 40 percent make things worse, not a very good track record. However, new insight about the brain is providing tools that can help leaders give feedback and performance reviews that make positive and lasting differences.

2. You Can Enhance One-on-One Communication with Those You Work With

Studying the brain helps us not only understand the brain itself but also develop common language to describe how the mind works. In Dr. David Rock's SCARF® model for team productivity (Rock, 2008), he explains that common language for brain functioning helps teams in many ways.

Since our brains are wired to respond to both social threats and rewards, such language helps us before, during, and after a threat in the workplace. It can help us know when we might set up an unintended threat and its potential impact on another (the "before"). For example, brain insight might prompt someone in a church setting—a youth pastor, for example—to pause

29

before he writes a harsh e-mail to a parent, because he realizes that he could set up a threat in that parent's emotional center.

Common language can also help us notice when a threat has occurred during an encounter with someone and how to manage emotions in our unique leadership setting. Let's say that the youth pastor sends the harsh e-mail anyway, which elicits angry words and hurt feelings from the parent. Instead of reacting immediately, the youth pastor uses brain insight to remind him that the parent is not allowing her thinking brain to quiet her emotional brain. As a result, the youth pastor gives the parent some time for her thinking to engage.

Finally, such language about the brain can help us understand what lies behind emotional situations that have already occurred in our work setting. It can help us understand and minimize the negative effect of those emotions. In the case above, such insight could prompt the youth pastor to use nonthreatening, brain-friendly language with the parent when she has cooled down (the "after") so they both can learn from the experience (Rock & Cox, 2012).

3. You Can Learn and Apply Proven and Effective Ways to Keep Cool under Pressure

Any leader who leads well must wisely manage his or her emotions. And most work environments require us to work with people who provide ample opportunity for emotions to flare. People get verbally angry at you; become passive-aggressive; perform poorly, which requires your intervention; or bring their family conflicts to the office. And when the emotionality of leaders takes over, they compromise their ability to lead well in these ways:

- impulse can overwhelm intention
- imagination gets pushed aside by instinct
- defensiveness stifles healthy positions
- automatic behavior shuts down reflective thought
- emotionality gets in the way of intentionality (Steinke, 2006, p. 20)

Often team members experience conflict, which requires a cool-headed, thoughtful leader's help. Wise leaders not only know how to control their emotions but also can help their team members control and process their own. Brain insight can help you navigate those emotional situations that can negatively impact productivity and team unity.

Christian leaders seek to control their emotions not simply for pragmatic reasons but for spiritual ones as well. One aspect of the fruit of the Spirit is self-control (Gal 5:23). As leaders, we honor the Lord through our spiritual responses in emotional situations. Understanding what happens in both our brain and our team members' brains can help us control those difficult emotions for God's glory and for organizational effectiveness.

4. You Can Improve Both Your Productivity and Your Team Members' Productivity

Brain insight can improve your team's productivity. Today's world moves lighting fast, and with the Internet's ubiquity your team probably experiences information overload. Work demands continue to grow even with faster, "time-saving" devices such as smart phones and tablet computers. The "always on" nature of those very devices actually cost companies millions of dollars each year through decreased productivity. In one study of US companies, employees reported that they usually worked fifteen minutes or fewer before getting distracted (O'Dell, 2011). All those interruptions mount up in lost productivity.

Also, in today's environment, distractive, intrusive thoughts often bombard our minds and keep us from working at our best. The more aware we become about these productivity drainers and how our brains can counter them, the more satisfied and productive our teams will become. In doing so we will live out what the Apostle Paul admonished us to do: "Whatever you do, do it from the heart for the Lord and not for people" (Col 3:23).

5. You Can Create Change More Effectively in Your Culture by Making It "Sticky"

Personal change precedes organizational change. Trying to force changes in others often backfires. People change when their values and beliefs change and when they don't feel threatened. Their values change when their minds change. So if you want to change people, you must understand their internal mental and emotional processes to create change. Lasting change will never occur apart from changing how people think and how they manage their responses to change.

Learning about how the brain works gives leaders keen insight into the inner worlds of their team members. The more they understand those processes, the more successful they'll become in creating the change they seek. Insight about effective change management may become one of the greatest contributions neuroscience will bring to Christian leaders.

Before I leave this chapter, I'm reminded about the death of one of the greatest modern-day Christian leaders, teachers, and thinkers, Dr. Howard Hendricks, professor at Dallas Theological Seminary. In early 2013, Howie, as he was affectionately called, went to be with the Lord.

His body finally yielded to age and Alzheimer's. Many of you have seen Alzheimer's ravage the mind of a friend or a loved one. I've seen it in my sweet aunt who lost the mental ability to put a spoon to her mouth or recognize her daughter. She knew the Lord, as did Dr. Hendricks, who influenced multiple thousands of us to walk closer to God, love God's word, and lead better.

I imagine an MRI just before his death would have revealed that Dr. Hendricks's once incredible mind had been reduced to something akin to Swiss cheese, the cruel effects this disease leaves. I'm eternally grateful for God's promise to his followers that in the great resurrection he will unite our souls to brand-new transformed bodies. I believe that our new bodies will include restored minds to those, who in Dr. Hendricks's case, were ravaged by the locusts of Alzheimer's. I look forward to the promise of heaven, where we will enjoy ever-expanding spiritual and mental growth as we continue to plumb the depths of an infinite God. I'm grateful that we are more than our brains; that once that last neuron fires, we continue to exist and will be with Jesus, our hope of glory.

A Picture Is Worth a Thousand Words

Neuroscience gives a strong brain basis for the truthfulness of that phrase—*a picture is worth a thousand words* (Ally & Budson, 2007). While thirty thousand fibers carry auditory data to our brains, a million do so for visual data (Rock & Page, 2009, p. 253). So, to aid learning and recall, I've intentionally used visual metaphors to capture not only the brain's parts and functions but also the four leadership domains as seen in this diagram, which you've seen before.

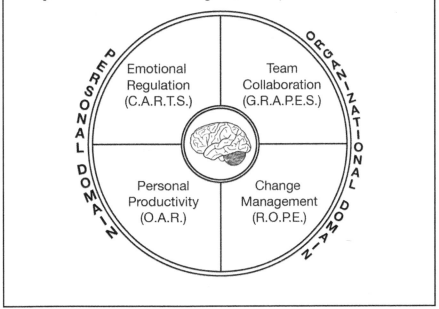

So before we delve into the four core leadership domains—emotional regulation, personal productivity, team collaboration, and change management—let's take a look at the parts of and players in this small, three-pound miracle called the brain.

The science behind...*Brain Surprise 3*: *If you feel drowsy, chewing gum may make you more alert.*

In a study published in 2013, researchers took participants through an exercise involving attention (Hirano et al., 2009). During the exercise they asked the participants to chew odorless and tasteless gum (to minimize any effect from taste or smell). Under an fMRI scanner they examined the parts of their brains that lit up,[1] or changed in activity. They discovered that chewing activated the brain's arousal and alertness centers. They surmised that the act of chewing potentially could lead to better brain functioning. Maybe your grammar school teacher who always told you to spit out your gum did you a disservice.

---

1.   Although the brain doesn't actually *light up* when it changes in activity, more oxygen-filled blood flows to that region, which the fMRI sees. For simplicity purposes, however, I'll use the popular term *lit up* in the book.

Section II

Meet Your Brain

Chapter 4

Meet Your Brain's Parts

Brain Surprise 4: *Botox treatments to your face can slow comprehension and might affect your emotional smarts.*

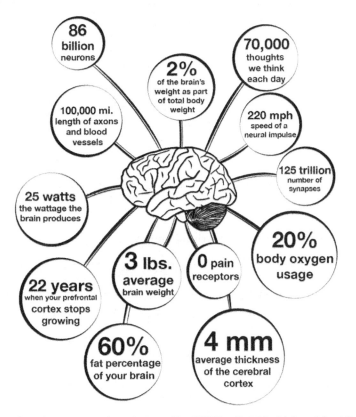

By the Numbers: Amazing Facts about the Brain That Will Blow Your Mind (adapted from Godwin & Cham, 2012). The number of synapses comes from Moore, 2010.

———

With the consistency of thick tofu and as wrinkled as a walnut, our brains reflect God's amazing, creative work. King David eloquently describes this in Psalms: "I give thanks to you that I was marvelously set apart. Your works are wonderful—I know that very well" (Ps 139:14). A contemporary writer put it this way, "If you look at the anatomy, the structure, the function, there's nothing in the universe that's more beautiful, that's more complex, than the human brain" (Schreiber, 2004).

To fully explain how the brain works would take the combined knowledge of all the world's past, present, and future neuroscientists. It would fill libraries and still be incomplete. So this chapter gives a simple overview of the brain's fundamental parts. As you read this chapter, it's not important to remember every detail. Rather, just try to get an overall grasp of the brain's makeup.

The brain's influence on leadership parallels how an iceberg appears. Just as we only see a small part of an iceberg from the surface, we also only see a limited part of how the brain influences outward leadership tasks, such as leading meetings, communicating, and coaching teams. Many unseen internal brain processes profoundly influence those surface functions and more.

So, let's first look at the brain from four different perspectives.

1. *Bottom to top* (called the triune brain)

2. *Left to right* (the brain's two hemispheres)

3. *Holistically* (a big-picture look at the brain's basic partitions, the lobes, and its fundamental building block, the neuron)

4. *Functionally* (activities that occur in various brain regions—the next chapter)

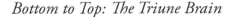

Bottom to Top: The Triune Brain

The Big Picture

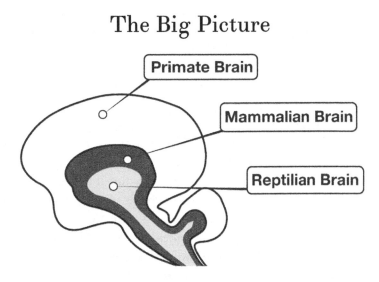

Neuroscientists call the bottom-to-top perspective the triune brain, which views the brain with three fundamental parts. I liken it to the three parts of a Tootsie Pop (see diagram): the stick, the Tootsie Roll inner core, and the outer candy shell. The Tootsie Pop stick represents the spinal cord. The small part of the stick stuck inside the candy represents what is called the "lizard" or "reptilian brain." The Tootsie Roll center represents the "mammalian brain" (also called the paleomammalian or limbic brain). And the candy coating represents the "primate" or "thinking brain" (also called the "neomammalian brain" or "neocortex").

The brain stem (the stick inside the candy) connects the spinal cord to the rest of the brain. The less-than-flattering "lizard brain" name comes from the fact that the lizard at your local pet shop has this part of the brain in common with us, although obviously there are still significant differences. The "lizard brain" works on autopilot to keep our body humming along whether we're awake or asleep and includes an important structure called the cerebellum. It controls body movement and involuntary processes like breathing, heart rate, balance, and blood pressure.

It also controls the release of important chemicals called neurotransmitters that rev up or slow down certain body systems so that we can survive when we feel threatened. This is our flight-or-fight response. Survival sometimes requires that we run from an actual tiger that's chasing us in the jungle to avoid being eaten. However, the brain can also respond in the same way when we face an imagined tiger (e.g., an angry board chair or a ticked-off church member). The brain stem is part of the body's autonomic nervous system that helps the body maintain its internal physiological functions. It's divided into two parts: the parasympathetic system, which slows down the body's systems (rest and digest), and the sympathetic system, which revs them up when facing threat (fight or flight).

The "mammalian brain" (the inner Tootsie Roll part) is the part of the brain we have in common with other mammals, like puppies, and is influenced by the primate brain and other higher brain structures. It regulates functions such as bonding, playing, and nurturing, and expressions, like shock, sorrow, and rejoicing. I've seen some of those attributes in our dog, Lulu. She's quite happy to see me when I come home from work. And when I scold her for something, her tail goes between her legs. She knows she did something wrong. And when she hears the doorbell ring, she gets into a state of alertness to protect me if it's a robber (at least I hope she does).

The "mammalian brain" also plays a role in pleasure and pain, flight and fight, and tension and relaxation. It includes structures that produce and control an important chemical involved in reward, the neurotransmitter called dopamine. We'll often see how this reward process impacts leadership. Two sets of important structures lie in this part of the brain: the limbic system (our emotional center) and the basal ganglia (where habits are stored).

Finally, the "primate brain," or our thinking brain (the candy coating), is the outmost part and sets us apart from the rest of creation. This is the crinkly, walnut-textured part we usually envision when we think about the brain. It's also called the cortex, which means "bark." Its hills and valleys are called gyri (hills) and sulci (valleys). These convolutions create more brain real estate and thus more working power. Both the "lizard" and the "mammalian" parts of the brain compose about 15 percent of the total brain and include many connecting neurons (brain cells) to the human brain. However, the "thinking" or "primate" brain encompasses 85 percent of the total brain. And the executive center of the brain that lies just behind our forehead makes up almost a third of the cortex. At this level God has uniquely given us the ability to think, process information, gain insight, and choose. It is the seat of intentionality, whereas the other two parts operate more from instinct.

In summary, the brain is made of three "brains":

- The "reptilian" or "lizard brain" is on autopilot and acts without thinking. It's worth noting that not only do lizards eat their young, but some boards also eat their leaders.

- The "mammalian brain" is the seat of emotions, also somewhat on autopilot.

- The "thinking" or "primate" brain," including the brain's executive center, is where thinking, analyzing, choosing, creating, planning, symbolizing, and observing occur.

Left to Right: The Brain's Hemispheres

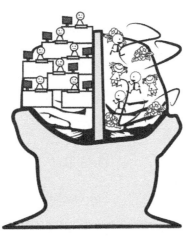

Another way to view the brain is from left to right (or right to left), much like how a walnut looks with its two hemispheres, or two sides. A large bundle of nerves, the corpus callosum, connects the hemispheres and acts like a super-highway to facilitate communication between both sides. Most, though not all, of the information that passes from one side to the other goes through this highway. These connections not only provide information flow but inhibit it as well to prevent one side from interfering with the other (McGilchrist, 2009, Kindle e-book loc. 530).

The brain works contralaterally, which means that the left side of the brain operates functions of the right side of the body, and vice versa. And each side of the brain tends to specialize, although neuroscientists are discovering that both sides can overlap to provide some of the same functions. In addition,

41

God gave us two of most every brain structure. In general the right side of our brain is more connected to the emotional center of our brain than is the left. As a result, we might say that it's the seat of our emotional and social self.

The following chart contrasts some basic functions each side performs. This chart only illustrates very generalized differences, and the science on these differences is still not definitive. For a detailed look at the differences, I recommend *The Master and His Emissary: The Divided Brain and the Making of the Western World* by Dr. Ian McGilchrist.

Left hemisphere	Right hemisphere
Concerned with the explicit	Concerned with the implicit
"And" stance	"Or" stance
Interested in the impersonal	Interested in the personal
Interested in the mechanical	Interested in the nonmechanical living
Detailed/sees the parts (trees)	Holistic/sees the whole (forest)
Explains	Describes
Processes the familiar	Processes the novel
Facts	Feelings
Narrow focus of attention	Broad focus of attention
Symbolic	Concrete
Logical	Intuitive
Concerned with the "what"	Concerned with the "how"
Verbal	Nonverbal
Sequential	Random
Language	Music

More used by managers

More used by leaders

Understands metaphors, a joke's punch line, emotional expression

Holistically: Picturing the Brain as a House

House ⇥ Brain
Rooms ⇥ Lobes and other structures
Building blocks ⇥ Neurons

Imagine the brain as a house made of billions of tiny bricks. Those fundamental building blocks or bricks of the brain are cells called neurons. They form massive connections through our brains. These bundles of bricks (neurons) form "rooms," called lobes, in the cortex that tend to specialize in certain functions (see previous image). Historically, neuroscientists have divided the brain into four lobes (matching sets on each side), but a fifth, the insula, is now considered by many to be a lobe as well. In each of these rooms, the brain performs certain activities or functions, just as we do in an actual house. We sleep in the bedroom, eat in the kitchen, relax in the den, and so on. We'll see in the next chapter that specific brain functions occur in the brain's rooms or structures.

However, not all our "sleeping" happens in the bedroom. Similarly, since the brain shows immense connectivity between its functions, while one function may occur in its normal region of the brain, another part may process that same information in a different way in another region.

Neurons: The Brain's Building Blocks

Neurons, the brain's fundamental building blocks, are the most sophisticated cells in the human body. As you read this sentence, millions of them are communicating to each other and to the rest of your body. They're so tiny that you could fit thousands of them into a period. They operate so fast that it takes much less time than the blink of your eyes to comprehend this sentence. Neuron cell bodies are what we think of as *gray matter*, yet part of the neuron is also white (the axon; see the diagram later in this chapter). They transfer and receive information, conduct electrical signals, and release chemicals called neurotransmitters. And neurons with similar functions tend to group together to form the brain's rooms (lobes).

Neurotransmitters Allow Neurons to Talk to Each Other

Without chemicals called neurotransmitters, neurons could not talk to each other or "fire," and our brains would be useless. Over one hundred neurotransmitters work in and on different parts of the brain. There are at least three neurotransmitters that traffic in our brains and emotions (Ratey, 2013, p. 5) that could significantly influence leadership. Dopamine (and a related neurotransmitter nor-epinephrine) influences attention, motivation, reward, alertness, and pleasure. Serotonin promotes a good mood, contributes to patience, and helps us delay gratification (Schweighofer et al., 2008). And oxytocin can help build trust among people, which is important for healthy teams.

Another group of brain cells are called glia cells, commonly considered the white matter. They outnumber neurons by as much as ten to one (Jabr, 2012). And what do they do? They serve as the brain's housekeepers, although recently neuroscientists have found them to take a more active role in actual brain processing as well (Koob, 2009). The name glia means "glue," and they hold the whole thing together, so to speak. They form insulation around the tail of a neuron (an axon), called myelin, which helps the brain process information quickly.

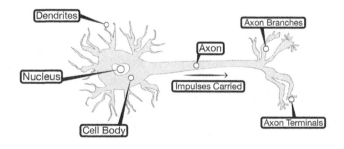

This image shows the basic parts of a typical neuron: the cell body, dendrites, axon, and the axon terminals. The space between one neuron's dendrites and another's axon terminals is called a synapse. John Medina in his book *Brain Rules* describes a neuron as being like an egg you've just stomped on (Medina, 2009, p. 53). The mess you create looks like a star. Stretch out one tip of the star and then at the end squish it with your thumb. So now you have two stars, the larger one at one end and the smaller one at the other, both connected by one long, thin line, similar to what we call the neuron's axon. The large egg squish would be called the neuron's cell body; its many points, dendrites, and the smaller thumb-squished points are the axon terminals. And when we learn, the dendrites get thicker, more numerous, and bushier like thick roots of a tree.

As amazing as a neuron is, its only task is to decide whether to fire or not to fire. When it fires (both a chemical and an electrical process), it sends an electrical signal or impulse down its axon. At the end of the axon lie terminals filled with small packets of neurotransmitters. The electrical impulse causes those packets to expel or spit out their neurotransmitters into the gap, the synapse, between the axon terminal of the presynaptic neuron (the "sending" neuron) and the dendrites/cell body of the postsynaptic neuron (the "receiving" neuron). They act like tiny couriers that communicate across this gap to the next neuron.

The receiving neuron can respond negatively to the couriers (called inhibition), or it can respond positively by evoking another electrical impulse to travel down its axon (called excitatory). After either of these, the couriers can scurry back into their packets in the originating neuron (called re-uptake) and begin the process all over again, or they can be broken down, making them inactive, and their components are then reused. Billions of neurons repeat this process over and over again, even now as you read this sentence. Drugs designed for issues like anxiety and depression work at this level either to encourage or inhibit this firing.

The old Mousetrap game I played as a child can help visualize this process. The game worked like this: I'd turn a crank that would cause a small plastic foot to kick a bucket that held a metal ball. When the metal ball spilled out of the bucket, it rolled down a trough, which started a chain reaction among the game's parts until eventually the mousetrap fell on the mouse.

Imagine this neuronal electrochemical process as a simplistic version of Mousetrap (yet so much more complicated). The ball (the electrical signal) travels down a trough (the axon) until it runs into a lever that knocks over a cup of water (the packets holding neurotransmitter couriers). The water (neurotransmitters) spills into the air (the synapses) onto some wires (dendrites) connected to a battery. They create an electrical current that turns on a small motor that dumps another ball that travels down a trough (electrical signal) to begin the whole process over again. Now imagine an ocean full of Mousetrap games doing this at lightning speed. In a similar way, billions of neurons connect to one another as they play their version of Mousetrap.

We could say that at a micro level, the neuron is the brain's decider and needs arms and legs, axons, to carry out its decisions. Our "heads" are in the gray matter and our "arms and legs" are in the white matter.

Until recently it was commonly thought that the brain doesn't develop new cells as we age. But new research has shown that our brains can grow new neurons. It's called neurogenesis. Neurogenesis is most common in the hippocampus, a key structure responsible for memory.

In contrast, *neuroplasticity* is the term used to describe how *existing* neurons reconfigure or rewire themselves. In one way this happens when we learn. What we pay attention to as we learn actually reconfigures the neuronal connections in our brain. The brain responds to patterns of behavior that get wired into us. Neuroplasticity also occurs when one part of the brain assumes functions it normally doesn't do by taking over the functions from a damaged part of the brain. For example, when blind people learn to read Braille, the brain uses real estate in the visual center of the brain to process information from their fingertips, usually processed in the part of the brain used for touch (Pascual-Leone et al., 2005).

When we learn, repeated thoughts about the same subject become mental maps that eventually become habits or deeply engrained beliefs. That's why reading, studying, and meditating upon scripture is so vital for a Christian. The more we focus on God's word, the more brain connections we make about his truth, thus reinforcing our values and beliefs. It's as if the Holy Spirit "rezones" our brains with God's truth. This change is called self-directed neuroplasticity. The Apostle Paul speaks to this change in Romans 12:2: "Don't be conformed to the patterns of this world, but be transformed by the renewing of your minds so that you can figure out what God's will is—what is good and pleasing and mature."

The Lobes: The Brain's Rooms

Information is processed starting at the back of your brain. As you move forward, you move from the sensory lobes in the back to the front, where what is sensed is "made sense of." For example, as you read this sentence, your occipital lobe in the back of your head receives data from your eyes. The letters and words are simply shapes on paper or a screen until processed at a deeper level. Your temporal lobes hold on to this information long enough for your frontal lobes to translate the pixels or shapes into words that you understand (I realize I'm oversimplifying).

Although the lobes form the outer part of your brain, they also dive deeper into it to connect to the other parts. Other "rooms" (subcortical structures) also lie beneath the neocortex, the outer covering. We'll look at some of the crucial ones when I explain the activities in those rooms in the next chapter.

The lobes perform these basic functions, although scientists are discovering more overlap for many functions.

Occipital lobe: receives and processes visual information such as color and motion

Parietal lobe: processes sensory information such as body awareness, environmental awareness, and touch

Temporal lobe: processes hearing, language, and memory; our brain's mental dictionary

Frontal lobe: the brain's executive center, which performs high-level thinking such as problem solving, decision making, and self-control; it also includes the premotor and motor cortex, which controls our intentional body movements; it's very crucial for effective leadership, as it also affects social interactions

Insular lobe: receives sensory input from what some call our second brain, the hollow organs like our intestines and heart; some neurons are located in these organs and help us experience our "gut feeling" and intuition; this lobe also processes smell and taste, especially related to the feeling and taste of disgust

Cortical Lobes

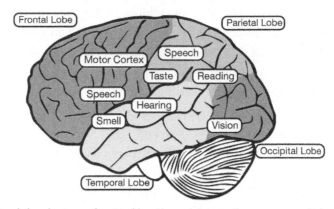

This diagram only loosely pictures functional locations and does not show a cutaway, which would reveal the insular lobe, where other processing occurs, such as smell.

Dr. Daniel Siegel, one of today's leading thought influencers on social cognitive neuroscience (how the brain affects how we relate), is known for his simple hand model of the brain. I find it quite helpful in bringing all the parts together.

> If you put your thumb in the middle of your palm and then curl your fingers over the top, you'll have a pretty handy model of the brain.... The face of the person is in front of the knuckles, the back of the head toward the back of your hand. Your wrist represents the spinal cord, rising from your backbone, upon which the brain sits. If you lift up your fingers and raise your thumb, you'll see the inner brainstem represented in your palm. Place your thumb back down and you'll see the approximate location of the limbic area (ideally we'd have two thumbs, left and right, to make this a symmetric model). Now curl your fingers back over the top, and your cortex is in place. (Siegel, 2010, Kindle e-book loc. 433)

So the brain is an amazingly complex gift to us from God. In the next chapter we will look at what goes on in the various rooms or parts of the brains. I call these activities *players*.

The science behind...*Brain Surprise 4*: *Botox treatments to your face can slow comprehension and might affect your emotional smarts.*

In one study, researchers injected Botox into participants' faces, temporarily paralyzing muscles used to express emotions usually evoked when reading (Havas et al., 2010). Then they read several sentences. The researchers discovered that some comprehension in the participants decreased due to the inability to form certain facial expressions. So our facial expressions help us comprehend better what we read. Botox injections to remove facial wrinkles may help our wrinkles, but not our brains.

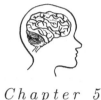

Chapter 5

Meet Your Brain's Players

Brain Surprise 5: *Boredom can shrink your brain.*

T he brain's activity operates somewhere between an imaginary playground and a battleground. The brain helps us enjoy the pleasure of a
sunset, the taste of a juicy peach, the humor in a joke, and the joy of relational
connection. It can help us feel calm, rested, focused, or fun. When I've seen
people's lives transformed by Christ, God fills my brain with these good experiences. Other times the brain feels like a battleground as we wrestle with
intrusive thoughts, anger, fear, dread, and disgust. For example, when I've
battled rejection by another, I wish I could have turned my brain off. It didn't
seem to serve me well at the time, yet it must work on the battlefield as well.

In this chapter I describe the brain's core process and explain the basic
activities, which I call *players*, in the brain's rooms. Although these metaphors
may greatly simplify things, they make more sense to the nontechnical reader
and make the concepts easier to remember as we apply them to leadership.

The Brain's Fundamental Organizational Principle and Operational Process

We can view the brain functioning with an overarching *organizational
principle* and a fundamental *operational process*. Dr. Evian Gordon, a neuroscientist, developed what he calls the INTEGRATE Model (Gordon et al.,
2008). This model describes the brain functioning around a basic organizing
principle, *Minimize Danger/Threat—Maximize Reward*. The terms *away* and

toward correspond to *danger/threat* and *reward*, and I'll often use the former terms through the book. The image that comes to mind for persons experiencing an *away* response would be their fists clenched as if to fight, their arms crossed, or their arms stretched out with their palms facing you as if to say, "Stop!" An image for a *toward* response might be someone with his or her arms extended to you as if to say, "Welcome!"

In other words, our brains tend to operate in a conscious and an unconscious mode that either seeks out reward (a toward response that is open, energized, and willing) or tries to avoid danger (an away response that is defensive, fearful, or closed). I think the Apostle Paul practiced this concept as he focused on the future: "Brothers and sisters, I myself don't think I've reached it, but I do this one thing: I forget about the things behind me and reach out for the things ahead of me. The goal I pursue is the prize of God's upward call in Christ Jesus" (Phil 3:13-14).

Minimize Danger/Threat—Maximize Reward: the brain's overarching operational principle that results in an away response (danger) or a toward response (reward).

The brain's overall *operational process* incorporates two subprocesses: the *X-system*, from the "x" in the word *reflexive* and the *C-system*, from the "c" in the word *reflective* (Lieberman, 2006). The X/C system is also called System 1 or System 2 in some circles. The X-system engages the parts of the brain that act spontaneously and impulsively, primarily our "lizard" and "mammalian brains." The C-system engages parts of the brain that act with intention and think before acting, our thinking center (the prefrontal cortex). This system also helps regulate our emotional reactions and can down-regulate the X-system. This chart briefly summarizes the fundamental differences.

Reflexive: X-System "low road"	Reflective: C-System "high road"
- impulsive	- intentional
- spontaneous	- controlled
- faster processing	- slower processing
- slower learning	- fast learning
- non-thinking	- thinking
- parallel processing	- serial proccesing
- not affected by mental load	- affected by mental load

When we combine the organizational principle with the operational processes, here's how our brain works, simply described: When we face danger (a threat), the brain processes information in two directions: the short route, sometimes called the low road (Johnson, 2003), and the long route, sometimes called the high road. The thalamus plays a critical role as a master information relay, or middleman, because all information from an external stimulus (or an internal self-generated one) flows through it. It shuttles the information about this stimulus to other parts of the brain. Here's what happens, all in a split second:

- Information about the threat first enters our brain through our sense organs and travels to the thalamus, the master relay, which shuttles information in two directions, toward the emotional center (short route) and toward the cortex and then to the higher thinking centers (long route). The information gets to the emotional center slightly quicker than it makes it to the thinking centers.

- As the thalamus relays the emotional content to the emotional center, in parallel it sends the nonemotional content through the memory center (the hippocampus) to the brain's thinking center (the prefrontal cortex) where it assesses and compares the new information to previously stored knowledge through its communication with the hippocampus.

- If it finds any prior knowledge, it sends it back to the memory center to incorporate this new information. Another relay mechanism called the RAS (reticular activating system) has a broader alerting function and relays information to all parts of the cortex.

- New mental maps then get combined with old ones and are then sent to memory storage.

- By this time, the emotional center may have already directed the body to respond. Even so, the thinking center will weigh in at some point to dampen the emotional center, confirm the emotional center's response, or direct the body to do something in response to the stimulus.

Here's an example of how that might work in real life (see the following diagram). Let's say I'm hiking in the woods and I see what I think is a snake I'm about to step on. My short route response, called the low road, quickly shuttles information to my emotional center (limbic system) and then to my peripheral nervous system. Among many body responses, the peripheral nervous system increases blood flow and respiration and instantaneously directs the muscles in my foot to avoid stepping on the snake. It helps me quickly respond to the perceived danger.

At the same time the long route process (the high road) sends that signal to my sensory cortex and then to my thinking center. It then recruits the brain's memory center to check for any data about snakes already stored in the brain's memory. It then sends its assessment back to the emotional center. Because my emotional center processed this as a snake, my body has already instantaneously reacted to direct me to plant my foot in a different place, any place but on the snake.

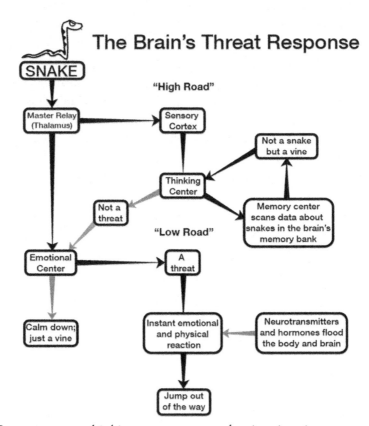

The Brain's Threat Response

However, as my thinking center assesses the situation, it compares it to maps already in the brain about a snake's color, size, movement, and so on. In relative terms it's slower than the low road, but only a fraction of a second slower. It may determine that the rattlesnake was simply a coiled vine that my emotional center interpreted as a snake. As a result, it begins to down-regulate my emotions and my body's response. I now don't have to worry because vines don't bite. Although my body is still tensed and my heart rate has jumped, my thinking center now tells my body it can calm down and not be alarmed. In diagram form it looks like the following. It's worth mention-ing that any diagram that attempts to describe how the brain works greatly simplifies what actually happens.

This same process can happen in a meeting with your board. Someone may say something that immediately feels like a threat (the low road, the X-system). But as your thinking center assesses what he says, it helps you realize that his words don't truly present a threat. So instead of internally stiffening up in fear or verbally reacting in defense, your brain can help you calm down (the high road, the C-system) so that you can stay fully engaged in the con-versation. The key is to pay attention to these internal signals. The low road provides the quick response, needed at times, and the high road response, although slower, more accurately assesses the situation.

This same process occurs with any intense emotion. Your brain will act the same way if you unexpectedly bump into Tom Cruise or Gwyneth Pal-trow at the grocery store or even if you don't know someone at a party. As with seeing a snake, your heart rate may jump, your respiration may increase, and your blood pressure may rise. Your brain's emotional center will initiate the stress response even if your "survival" is not threatened, although not looking dumb in front of Tom might qualify as a survival situation.

In my years in ministry leadership, I've sometimes taken the low road and reacted in anger to a staff person, become defensive at someone's critical comment, or acted like a jerk in the heat of the moment. In those cases, my brain's X-system overrode its C-system, and I gave in to my emotions. I didn't wait long enough for my thinking brain to inform my actions so that I could respond in a Spirit-directed way.

When the X-system gets overloaded, two processes occur that can sup-press the C-system: hormones enter our bloodstream and neurotransmitters flood our brain. Whereas neurotransmitters are chemical messengers that move along our nervous system, hormones are chemical transmitters that move through our blood system. Some molecules can even act as both.

When our X-system gets overloaded, we can respond in these ways.

- Emotions can inhibit impulse control.

- The reactive parts of our brain can take over and we can become defensive.

- Objectivity can diminish.

- We don't listen well to others because our brains can't concentrate on others' viewpoints without prematurely framing our own responses.

And the writer of Proverbs speaks to what happens when we act impulsively rather than respond thoughtfully:

Ignorant desire isn't good; rushing feet make mistakes. (19:2)

It is a snare to say rashly, "It is holy," and only reflect after making the promise. (20:25)

Do you see people who are quick to speak? There is more hope for fools than for them. (29:20)

The Players in the Brain's Rooms: Activities That Happen There

The more we understand how our brain works, the better we can leverage it to help us lead more effectively. It's also worth remembering that we engage many parts of our brain as we walk with the Lord. We learn about the Bible when we use our thinking brain. We emotionally connect with the Lord when we engage our emotional centers. Our visual centers help us envision his greatness, majesty, and goodness and help us visually connect to the Bible's vivid imagery and to historical settings.

Next I describe some key brain functions that apply to life in general and leadership in particular, what I've called players in the brain's rooms. I don't focus on the scientific names, although I provide the names. It's important, however, to understand how these functions work because I'll refer to them in the chapters that follow when I unpack the four leadership domains. I've greatly simplified what happens in these regions. Different parts of the brain can also share these roles.

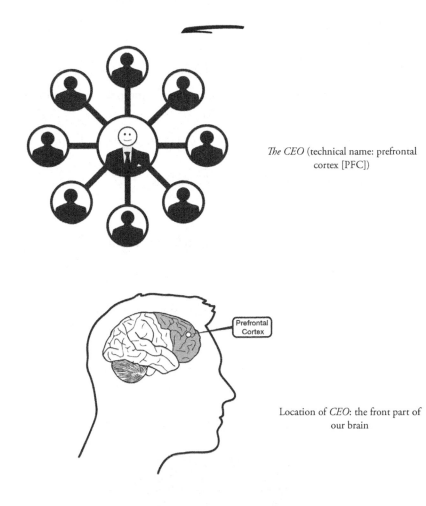

The CEO (technical name: prefrontal cortex [PFC])

Location of *CEO*: the front part of our brain

The *CEO* (PFC) is the brain's director and delegator. Our complex thinking functions and decisions originate from here, making it crucial for leadership. It forms a major part of the frontal lobe along with the premotor and the motor cortex, which direct our physical movements. The *CEO* is the brain's executive center, where high-level decision making, working memory, planning, and abstract thinking occur. It constantly manipulates and draws upon collections of memories in our brains that I've called maps. David Rock says that the *CEO* performs five core functions related to those brain maps:

1. *Recalling*, when it searches for and retrieves relevant maps.

2. *Deciding*, when it chooses the maps it wants to use.

3. *Understanding*, when it draws information from those maps.

4. *Memorizing*, when it holds those maps in memory long enough for new information to be stored.

5. *Inhibiting*, when it ignores irrelevant maps. (Rock, 2009, p. 47)

However, our *CEO* also has some limitations.

1. It tires easily.

2. It has limited storage capacity, like RAM in a computer.

3. It's very fussy.

For your *CEO* to work most effectively, the environment has to be just right, much like Goldilocks in the fairy tale where everything had to be "just right." I explain this in more detail later, but essentially this "just right" state requires a balanced amount of neurotransmitters, not too much and not too little.

Another important key involves processing. The *CEO* processes information serially in contrast to in parallel. That is, as part of the C-system, it processes bits of information one after the other (serial) instead of several at the same time (parallel). For example, look at this picture. What do you see?

You can only see one object at a time, either the vase or the two faces. You can't see both at once, even though we think we can. We're simply switching very quickly between each image. However, when we try to process too much information at once, the *CEO*'s serial processing nature can result in mental processing bottlenecks that in turn can lead to unfinished thoughts and tasks.

An old, yet funny sitcom episode illustrates this concept. In one *I Love Lucy* episode, Lucy and Ethel worked at a chocolate candy factory. As the conveyor belt moved unwrapped pieces of candy one at a time in front of them, their job was to wrap each piece in a candy wrapper. Things went smoothly until the conveyor belt sped up. When that happened, everything fell apart. Lucy and Ethel began to stuff candy into their shirts and cram it into their mouths. Search for this video on the Internet and you'll get a good laugh and see what happens when serial processing overloads us. In a similar way, when we attempt many mental tasks at once, our thinking degrades, accuracy drops, we focus on the urgent instead of the important, we forget things, and the quality of future decisions gets muddied. In a later chapter I talk about the downside of multitasking.

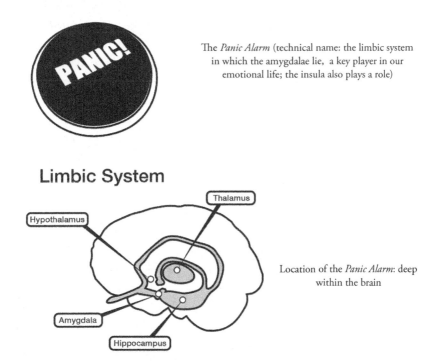

The *Panic Alarm* (technical name: the limbic system in which the amygdalae lie, a key player in our emotional life; the insula also plays a role)

Limbic System

Location of the *Panic Alarm*: deep within the brain

Many parts of the brain influence our emotions, but the *Panic Alarm* (the limbic system, especially the amygdala) contributes the most. The word *limbic* means "edge," and it got its name because it lies on the edge between the outer part of the brain and other important internal structures. In general, its primary structures include the amygdalae, the hippocampus, and the hypothalamus. The *Panic Alarm* strongly influences the X-system.

The amygdalae (I will use the singular form amygdala going forward) are two almond-shaped structures that for several reasons play a critical role in our emotions. The amygdala is constantly on the lookout for problems and receives sensory input from many other parts of the brain. It's involved in consolidating emotional memories, especially those related to fear, yet the research on this topic is somewhat unclear.

Both the hippocampus and the amygdala are involved in memory, the former primarily for facts and the latter for emotions. For example, your hippocampus helps you remember the names of your board members. The amygdala tells you which ones you like. Because the amygdala is so highly connected to other parts of the brain, when it gets overly activated (the *Panic Alarm* goes off), it can diminish our *CEO's* thinking ability and affect our leadership.

An external real or perceived threat, a memory, imagining ourselves in a threatening situation, or even anticipating a threat can incite our *Panic Alarm*. The flight-flight-freeze-appease response originates from here. It's also vital in helping us form healthy emotional attachments, especially at an early age.

Another component of the limbic system, the hypothalamus, acts as a controller to the master hormone gland, the pituitary gland. When we're under stress it causes the adrenal glands to release the stress hormone cortisol into our bloodstream and neurotransmitters into our brain. Our body reacts very quickly to the neurotransmitter release but slower to the hormonal release. And chronic stress can damage our body and even kill neurons in the hippocampus. However, since the hippocampus is one of the few structures that can grow neurons, called neurogenesis, when stress decreases and cortisol levels out, the brain can regrow neurons here.

Another significant part of the brain, the insula, also influences emotions and informs the amygdala. It maps our body's internal feelings (called interoception) by receiving continuous input from over 100 million neurons that line our hollow organs, like our heart and intestines (Armour, 2004). It takes this information and represents how we feel in relation to our outside environment. Intuition is affected by this so-called second brain (Hadhazy, 2010). It can give us a "gut" feeling, butterflies in our stomach, or a "heartfelt sense" we sometimes feel about something or someone. It's also finely tuned to feel disgust and to sense unfairness.

I believe God used my insula to help me make a difficult decision years ago. I had been leading a poorly performing staff member that I had hoped I could reform to fit our culture. I kept telling myself that I could change him. But nothing seemed to work. I thought I needed to release him, but I just couldn't seem to pull the trigger. However, when I woke up suddenly in the middle of the night, I knew in my gut I had to release him. I believe the Holy Spirit used my insula to help me make that decision.

Related to the insula, it's interesting to note that although the Bible never uses the word *brain*, it often uses the word for *bowels* to refer to the deep interior of our heart, soul, and mind. Although the biblical writers didn't explicitly understand the inner workings of the brain, God gave them keen insight into how our bodies and brains actually worked in real life.

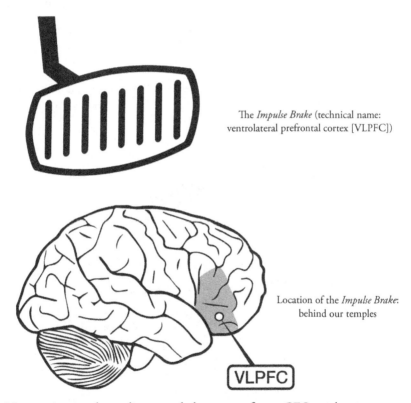

The *Impulse Brake* (technical name: ventrolateral prefrontal cortex [VLPFC])

Location of the *Impulse Brake*: behind our temples

VLPFC

Neuroscientists have discovered that part of our *CEO* works as an emotional brake, a key to impulse control (Cohen et al., 2011). It operates in a top-down fashion that can help calm our emotions and impulses, which I'll discuss in detail in the next chapter on emotional regulation.

Our *Impulse Brake* (ventral lateral prefrontal cortex) works somewhat like this: When something in our environment feels threatening (or we think about something threatening), the brain's *Error Detector* (see image) goes off and can recruit the *Impulse Brake* (VLPFC) to quiet the *Panic Alarm*. It also helps us control our intrusive thoughts, motor responses, and our ability to say no to that second piece of chocolate cake. It even helps us resist the impulse to buy that tool at the hardware store that we want but don't need. It helps us manage our money better by helping us say no to poor money decisions (Cohen et al., 2012). And just as muscles can tire with use, it also tires easily. If you've had to resist the impulse to buy, act upon your emotions, or do something you shouldn't, you'll need to give yourself a break to recharge in an environment where you don't have to continue to resist more impulses.

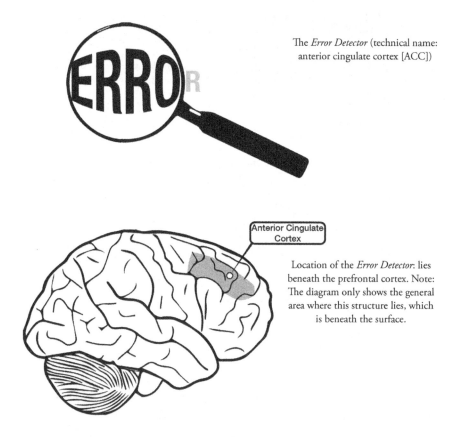

The *Error Detector* (technical name: anterior cingulate cortex [ACC])

Anterior Cingulate Cortex

Location of the *Error Detector*: lies beneath the prefrontal cortex. Note: The diagram only shows the general area where this structure lies, which is beneath the surface.

The brain's *Error Detector* (anterior cingulate cortex) lies beneath the *CEO* at the front of our forehead. It's at the cusp of the C-system and the X-system and highly connected to our emotional and motor centers. It detects error and monitors conflict, alerting the thinking center when it senses something isn't right.

It detects conflicting priorities, preferences, or beliefs and activates when something it experiences doesn't jibe with expectations. Like a security system, it monitors what's happening in your world for any errors that arise from what you would expect from your current experience. By monitoring how things are currently, it helps our actions stay in sync with our intended goals or actions.

If it senses something isn't right, a discrepancy, it alerts the *CEO* (the C-system) to get involved and help make some sense of the situation, bring belief in line with behavior, or direct the body to take some action. It's also involved with processing pain and the emotional distress associated with pain. However, it can become too sensitive and fire too often, like a spellchecker that indicates that you misspelled every word you type, even though the words are correct. When that happens, it can get the *Panic Alarm* too involved. People who struggle with obsessive-compulsive disorder have an *Error Detector* and an *Accountant* (see image on p. 65) that are too sensitive.

For example, many years ago I was talking with a board member about my performance at work. I'll call him John. As John talked, he complimented me on my performance, yet his body language seemed to convey something different. Something inside me made me feel that he was not sincere with his compliments. His words didn't fit his body language. At that point I believe my *Error Detector* had alerted me to this conflict I felt. My hunch was later confirmed by his actions. His compliments were not sincere. In fact, shortly thereafter he began a plan to oust me from my position.

The brain's *Error Detector* lies between the frontal lobes and the limbic system and acts as a mediator between our feelings and thoughts. A good way to visualize how the *Error Detector* works with the *CEO* and the *Panic Alarm* is to imagine a child's seesaw. In the following diagram, on the left is the *Panic Alarm*. On the right is the *CEO*. The *Error Detector* is at the center, acting like the fulcrum. Like a fulcrum beneath a seesaw, it helps balance and control what happens between the brain's *Panic Alarm* and the *CEO* (Newberg & Waldman, 2010, Kindle e-book loc. 2097).

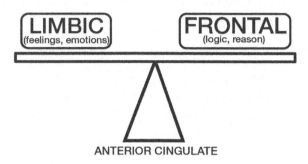

Like an air traffic controller, the *Error Detector* shuttles information between the two. If you get too emotional (the left side of the seesaw goes up), the amygdala activates and can hinder the *CEO*.

However, when the *Impulse Brake* is engaged, the *Error Detector* can shuttle new information to turn down the *Panic Alarm*.

The *Error Detector* is also involved in intuition and social awareness. In fact, it's larger in women, which may explain why they tend to have more social skills than men (Newberg & Waldman, 2010, Kindle e-book loc. 904). Additionally, we engage this part of the brain when we sense that something is not morally or ethically right (Greene et al., 2004). And some neuroscientists believe our *Error Detector* plays a critical role in our spiritual practices (Newberg & Waldman, 2010, Kindle e-book, loc 741).

Finally, the brain's *Error Detector* may provide the link between our conscious and our unconscious thinking, like what happened when I spoke to John about my performance. My conscious brain heard what he was saying, but something in my unconscious made me feel that he was disingenuous. Because it picked up on subtle unconscious signals, I believe the Holy Spirit used that part of my brain to give me a truer read on reality and prepare me for the conflict that soon ensued. I believe scripture points to this inner sense in these verses.

> Dear friends, don't believe every spirit. Test the spirits to see if they are from God because many false prophets have gone into the world. (1 John 4:1)

> The Beroean Jews were more honorable than those in Thessalonica. This was evident in the great eagerness with which they accepted the word and examined the scriptures each day to see whether Paul and Silas' teaching was true. (Acts 17:11)

The *Accountant* (technical name: orbitofrontal cortex [OFC])

Location of the *Accountant*: centered right behind our eyes

Orbitofrontal
Cortex

The *Accountant* (orbitofrontal cortex) of the brain acts like an accountant or analyst that keeps track of memories by calculating the pros and cons of a pending decision. It produces a mental balance sheet of the risks and rewards for the action center of the brain (Pilay, 2011, Kindle e-book loc. 677). It also tracks the emotional value of experiences, what we like and don't like, and our preferences and values (Wolpert, 2010). It remembers the consequences of past behavior by helping us recall that behavior.

It brings emotional memory into decision making as it serves as the working memory for our emotions. This is very important because if we can't recall the emotional consequence of a pending decision, we lose an important factor that can help us make good decisions. For example, when I was a kid, I got deathly sick after eating a popcorn ball. Although the popcorn ball may have had nothing to do with my sickness, to this day I won't eat one. My *Accountant* has kept track of that emotional experience and it still comes into play every time I see a popcorn ball. Yet I'm not stuck with an aversion to popcorn balls, nor are any of us stuck in values or patterns based on old information. If I tried popcorn balls, I'd probably find that I could learn to like them.

Self-reflection and thinking about ourselves, our preferences and values, what we like and don't like, and our motivations and desires also lie in our brain's *Accountant*. Related to our *Accountant*, the brain region immediately above and below our *Accountant*, the medial prefrontal cortex (mPFC), helps us *mentalize*, the ability to step inside the shoes of another to see things from his or her perspective.

When we are not focusing on a specific task, this part of the brain engages in daydreaming or mind wandering. The *Accountant* also thinks about what others are thinking. It's like a default mode we revert to if something doesn't demand our attention.

The *Automatic Transmission* (technical name: basal ganglia)

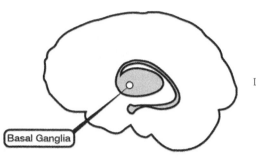

Location of the *Automatic Transmission*:
deep inside the brain

Basal Ganglia

The basal ganglia, the brain's habit center that I've coined the *Automatic Transmission*, is a collection of structures highly connected to the brain's master relay, the thalamus. When you learn a new habit or routine, it's stored in your *Automatic Transmission*. When the right cues are present, they trigger these habits automatically. It's also a very energy-efficient structure compared to your *CEO* because it operates on autopilot. It operates in the background because our habits have been embedded into our brains over time. For example, if you've driven for many years, you can drive and do other tasks at the same time, like listening to the radio, without having to think about driving. And because habits are so deeply ingrained, they're hard to break.

Our *Automatic Transmission* is also very fast and automatic because it doesn't have to take time to think. In fact, one study showed that 40 percent of what we do each day is a habit (Neal et al., 2006). Your *Automatic Transmission* also receives dopamine from the *Rewarder-Motivator* (see p. 69), which is key to creating new habits and skills. That part of the brain rewards you with a pleasant feeling as you form a habit. And when we do something that feels good, it puts us into a state to want to repeat it. Although you need to think a lot when you initially form a habit, as you engrain it into your mind you don't have to think about it as much. The habit becomes automatic and quick. Like a car's automatic transmission, the basal ganglia automatically shifts our attention as the brain demands. Dopamine actually acts like its transmission fluid to help our brains shift our attention (Ratey, 2013, p 152).

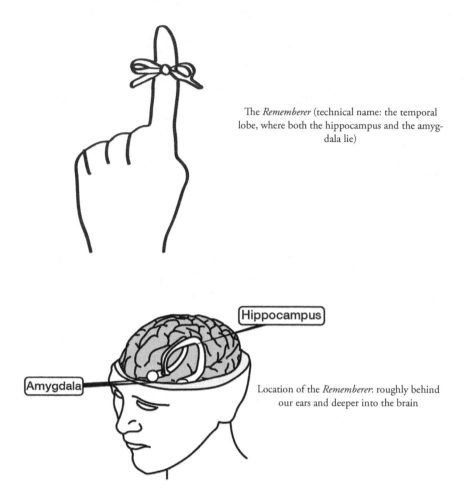

The *Rememberer* (technical name: the temporal lobe, where both the hippocampus and the amygdala lie)

Hippocampus

Amygdala

Location of the *Rememberer:* roughly behind our ears and deeper into the brain

Your *Rememberer*, the hippocampus, is a seahorse-shaped structure extremely important for converting short-term information into long-term memory. It moves memories into massive "mental filing cabinets" located all over the brain, not just in one location. Like a way station, it assembles input and data fragments from various parts of the brain. It bundles and links this new information to previously stored information and in turn creates new memories, or maps. It helps bind together various parts of memory traces and pushes those memories into the rest of the brain as long-term memory through a process called consolidation. This process occurs while we are both awake and asleep.

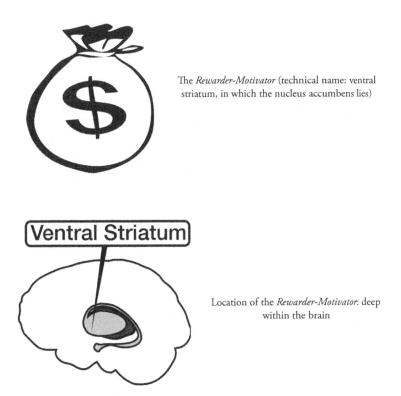

The *Rewarder-Motivator* (technical name: ventral striatum, in which the nucleus accumbens lies)

Location of the *Rewarder-Motivator*: deep within the brain

Your *Rewarder-Motivator* (ventral striatum) sounds like what it does. It rewards and motivates us by using neurotransmitters. It's richly connected to your *Panic Alarm*, especially the amygdala. Its neurons receive lots of neurotransmitters, such as dopamine and serotonin, from rewarding experiences, which in turn promote learning and habit formation. When we learn something or create a habit, it feels good because learning is both rewarding and motivating. What gets rewarded gets learned. Chocolate, coffee, drugs, and stress can affect the *Rewarder-Motivator's* performance.

So in this chapter we've looked at both the brain's organizational principle (minimize danger/threat—maximize reward) and its operational process (the X- and C-systems). I also described some of the brain's critical activities that have bearing on leadership, which I called "players." I've repeated them here, but only the images that picture the activity. Look at the images and see how well you can recall and define them.

The Brain's Fundamental Players

How did you do? I bet you were able to remember most if not all of them. In the pages that follow, I'll often refer back to them.

As we move into the next section, it's helpful to know why neuroscience knowledge is exploding today. It's primarily due to the advent of the functional MRI (fMRI). This use of the traditional MRI, which was first used in 1973, has opened up the doors to brain research since neuroscientists first began to use fMRI in 1992. It shows what neighborhoods of the brain light up (are active) during mental activities by marking where the brain recruits oxygen-filled blood (oxygenated blood). It takes multiple sliced pictures (think slices of bread) and then puts them back together into one image.

Essentially it takes a picture of the brain thinking at points in time. In fMRI images, colorful blobs highlight the brain's activity at the point it was taken. Based on these observations, neuroscientists then infer from this internal understanding to augment their understanding of what actually happens in real life. By combining what happens in specific brain regions with what happens in the brain's larger networks of regions, we're learning more about how the brain impacts leadership. And as other neuroscientists perform similar research and corroborate the findings, it increases our confidence that the findings correspond to real-life experience.

The science behind...*Brain Surprise 5*: *Boredom can shrink your brain.*

One researcher examined the importance of oxygen and blood flow to the brain as it related to boredom (Saunders, 1996). When we feel bored we don't get as much oxygen and blood flow. When the brain lacks engagement over long periods of time (we are bored), dendrites can atrophy. When that happens, we can lose brain real estate. So, the next time you get bored, find something that interests you. There may be a neuroscience basis to the sayings, "Variety is the spice of life" and, "Use it or lose it."

Section III

Brain-Based Leadership Competencies

Chapter 6

Using Your Brain to Stop the Emotional Freight Train

Brain Surprise 6: *If you put a pencil sideways in your mouth and pull your lips back, your brain will make you feel happier.*

As a pastor-leader, I've enjoyed leading, teaching, and helping people find purpose for living and navigate life's difficulties. Although some people assume pastors live problem-free lives, we're much like everyone else. Our vocation doesn't insulate us from life's U-turns and disappointments. Several years ago I faced a defining moment in my ministry. The ruling board in our church took a different philosophical direction, and because I could not embrace it, I resigned my position with no place to go. Such a move placed me in a precarious vocational position.

As a result, my thoughts became very negative about my experience. The natural tendency to which our brains default, the proverbial "glass is half-empty" mentality, often overwhelmed my thinking (Baumeister et al., 2001). The uncertain circumstances seemed to overwhelm the good God was doing in my life that although was objectively true, I could not seem to appreciate. My mind felt like a child's playground toy, the teeter-totter. My thoughts would be negative one minute and then swing to the positive for a short time and then swing back to the negative again. I mostly found myself mired in a negative funk. Fortunately, I began to learn how the brain affects our emotions and began to apply concepts to emotional control. They worked.

In this chapter we will look at five brain-based concepts that can help us manage our emotions by helping us avoid popping our tops or stuffing our emotions and imploding from within.

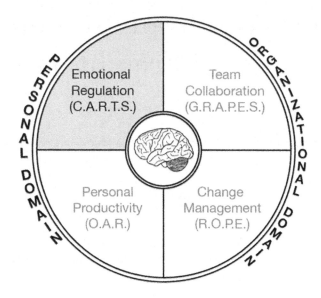

Perhaps the place to start is to ask, "What are emotions and what causes them?" From a brain perspective, an emotion, whether negative or positive, is a process that begins with some stimulus. Something outside our minds can start the process: you get a nasty e-mail from someone in your church. Or something inside our minds: while daydreaming your thoughts wander to the criticism you got last week from a participant in the Bible study you lead or you anticipate something that might occur tomorrow.

The brain interprets this stimulus as a threat, in the case of a negative emotion, which taps into events and memories of past events. The process actually starts before we become aware of the emotion. In less than half a second we feel the emotion that had already begun to well up in our sub-conscious mind. Your brain sends neurotransmitters and hormones through your nervous system and bloodstream, respectively, to create physiological responses like increased heart rate, dilated pupils, and that *anxious* feeling. This process evokes various thoughts and feelings (our actual perception of the emotion). As a result, physiological and cognitive responses will feed back into our brain and impact the emotion over time unless we consciously stop it. In the previous chapter we saw that Dr. Evian Gordon calls this process the INTEGRATE Model (Gordon et al., 2008) around the brain's basic organizing principle: minimize danger/threat—maximize reward. His model further explains what happens within the brain when we experience an emotion. (Also see the diagram on p. 54 when I explained what happens in our brains when we think we see a snake.)

- stimulus (threat or reward in some internal or external context) >>
- emotion (at an unconscious level, starts within one-fifth of a second) >>
- feeling (we become conscious of the emotion within half a second) >>
- thinking (attention, assessment, interpretation, decision) >>
- response (an action in response to the feeling and our assessment of the situation)

Every emotion follows this simplified pattern. So in this chapter we'll look at how we can keep emotions like fear or anger from erupting into words or actions that we wish we could take back, the low road we discussed earlier. The low road, you'll recall, is fast. We need speed when we're truly in danger and must react without thinking (slam on the brakes to avoid a wreck). But in leadership situations we want to take the "high road" to allow the brain's *CEO* (prefrontal cortex) to control our behavior and speech. The following story illustrates how leaders must choose between the high road and the low road every day.

Several years ago, before I learned about the brain, I used a movie clip to illustrate a point in a talk that I had just delivered in the first Sunday morning service at my church. It came from an R-rated movie, but the clip didn't include any offensive material. Immediately after my sermon a woman accosted me and criticized me for using it. She felt offended because it came from the R-rated movie. At that point I was faced with two choices. I could have allowed my *Panic Alarm* (limbic system) to control me, and I could have verbally reacted by pointing out her narrow-mindedness. Had I done that, I would have wounded her and hurt a relationship as well as made myself look like a jerk. Or I could have taken the high road by cooperating with the Holy Spirit's desire that I use my *CEO* and practice Proverbs 21:29, which says, "the virtuous think about the path ahead."

If I took the low road, not only would I damage the relationship, but also I would have robbed my *CEO* of the energy it needed for me to be at my best at the second service when I spoke again. If I took the high road, I could listen attentively to her to understand her viewpoint and hold my tongue. Fortunately I made the latter choice and kept the relationship intact. I also learned a valuable lesson. Every time I show a clip from a potentially objectionable movie, I now give a short caveat to explain that I don't necessarily endorse the content of the movie.

This experience illustrates sit.uations we face where we should monitor and manage our emotions. However, such control can feel much like a tug-of-war between our *CEO* and our *Panic Alarm*. Remember, we have limited mental resources to deal with daily demands as leaders, and both parts of our brain vie for those same resources. (Interestingly, some recent research suggests that self-control may not be a limited resource in the way it's currently viewed [Inzlicht et al., 2014]. More research is needed though.) Self-control doesn't come easily. The Apostle Paul describes it as a *spiritual* tug-of-war when he writes in Romans 7:15: "I don't know what I'm doing, because I don't do what I want to do. Instead, I do the thing that I hate."

When our *Panic Alarm* activates and our *Impulse Brake* does not moderate it, whatever the reason, problems begin. We react to others, cut them off, or drive our emotions inward. While we need our *Panic Alarm* to take charge when we're truly threatened, we don't need it to run wild when in a heated meeting at the office or while in a conflict with a staff member or someone in our family. At that point we need the *CEO* to direct our behavior.

So how do we help the *CEO* control the *Panic Alarm* when in the heat of the moment? First we must realize that God has given us the ability to exercise self-control. He says that spiritual fruit gives evidence that the Holy Spirit is active in our lives. Several aspects of this fruit directly imply emotional control: "But the fruit of the Spirit is love, joy, *peace, patience,* kindness, goodness, faithfulness, *gentleness,* and *self-control.* There is no law against things like this" (Gal 5:22-23, emphasis added). Several other verses about emotional control include the following:

- "A person without self-control is like a breached city, one with no walls." (Prov 25:28)

- "You have heard that it was said to those who lived long ago, *Don't commit murder*, and all who commit murder will be in danger of judgment. But I say to you that everyone who is angry with their brother or sister will be in danger of judgment." (Matt 5:21)

- "Fools show all their anger, but the wise hold it back." (Prov 29:11)

However, we can't separate how our brains work from how the Holy Spirit works in us to create change in our hearts and in our character. Emotional control is not a passive process. It requires our intentional effort to work with the Holy Spirit. We can't assume that because we love the Lord he will automatically stop us from blowing up at somebody or driving our anger inward. Spirit-led emotional control has a brain basis as well. In fact, scientists have discovered what many have known a long time: faith actually helps us become more self-controlled (Rounding et al., 2012).

God has wired our brains to support his promises, such as this one: "No temptation has seized you that isn't common for people. But God is faithful. He won't allow you to be tempted beyond your abilities. Instead, with the temptation, God will also supply a way out so that you will be able to endure it" (1 Cor 10:13). God built into our brains a systematic Spirit-directed "way out" from the temptation. We don't have to yield to our impulses. Even in the most extreme situations, God promises that he will give us everything we need even to turn the other cheek (Matt 5:39) rather than retaliate.

Let's unpack a bit more how our brains help with self-control.

Fear, conscious and unconscious, is prompted by the amygdala in our *Panic Alarm*. The brain naturally focuses on problems and the negative. It overestimates threats and underestimates opportunities. In fact, two-thirds of the brain cells in our amygdala are primed for negativity and fear (Hanson, 2010). Negative networks in our brain outweigh positive ones by five to one (Baumeister et al., 2001). And negative emotions are more easily consolidated (made more permanent) into our long-term memory than positive emotions. When researchers showed angry faces to volunteers lying in an fMRI scanner, their amygdala lit up (Whalen et al., 2001). It didn't when they saw positive ones. When we feel fearful, our *CEO* and the *Panic Alarm* engages in this tug-of-war for our limited mental resources. And because our *CEO* tires easily, it often gives in to the *Panic Alarm*; hence a good reason to get rest and adequate amounts of sleep (Batista, 2009).

Fear can even be subconscious, especially if we're surrounded by bad news, critical people, or if our self-talk is constantly negative (Morris et al., 1999). Because our *Panic Alarm* connects to so many parts of the brain, when it's activated, it impacts several functions of our *CEO,* like memory, decision making, motivation, and attention.

Again, it's important to realize that we do have control over what we do with our emotions. In the 1980s some researchers performed an experiment to determine how much control we can exert over our impulses to act. The experiments involved observing participants move their fingers or wrists when they felt like it, as the participants watched a clock (Pychyl, 2011). The researchers then measured three things:

1. the exact time they were consciously aware of their urge to flex;

2. the moment they recorded electrical activity in the brain (called the "readiness potential"); and

3. the moment they recorded electrical activity in the muscle in the wrist.

They discovered some unexpected findings. Activity in the brain's motor center preceded their conscious awareness by about one-third of a second. The scientists then repeated the experiment and asked participants to stop once they became aware of their urge to move their wrist. They were able to stop, indicating that they had a choice to control their behavior. They were able to exercise veto power over their impulse to move their wrist. In other words, the experiment showed a key impulse control insight. When we feel an emotional impulse to do something, we do have the ability to recognize the impulse before we act on it, although it's a small window, and the ability to not act on it. The experiments indicated that we have conscious choice to *not* do something (i.e., say something when we feel anger). The researches then coined the phrase "free won't." It's a function of the *Impulse Brake* discussed in the prior chapter.

James captures this idea in these verses: "Know this, my dear brothers and sisters: everyone should be quick to listen, slow to speak, and slow to grow angry. This is because an angry person doesn't produce God's righteousness" (Jas 1:19-20). When we feel anger (or any other emotion) and the impulse to say something or do something, God has given us the ability to *not* act on that impulse. We have "free won't."

When we practice self-control, we get many benefits, as the following study revealed. In 1972 researchers at Stanford University performed a famous study on children and their ability to control their impulses (Bennett, 2012, and Mischel et al., 1972). Many have since repeated the study. Young children were placed in a room with a desk, a chair, a plate, and a marshmallow. They were told that if they didn't eat the marshmallow, in a few minutes when the researcher returned, they could have two marshmallows. The researcher then left the room while a camera captured what the children did.

It's a funny and enlightening video that pictures how we struggle to control our impulses. If you search for this video on the Internet, you're in for a good chuckle. One child stared at the marshmallow. One picked it up and smelled it. Another just touched his tongue to it. Another one couldn't resist. She ate it. These children were followed into adulthood and the researchers discovered that the ones who could delay gratification made better grades, were more successful, healthier, and proved better at staying in relationships (Shoda et al., 1990). Later studies showed that trust in the researcher also played a factor. So, impulse control carries long-lasting benefits, not to mention immediate ones.

So how do we do it?

That's where the acronym CARTS comes in. In this chapter I use the image of a simple wooden cart with a pile of unhappy faces in it.

Imagine your emotions as something tangible you can actually pick up and hold. By applying the insights that follow, you can put your emotions "in a cart" and "haul them away" by engaging your *Impulse Brake* and quieting your *Panic Alarm*.

The letters in the acronym CARTS represent specific choices we can make to manage our emotions.

- **C**hange your circumstances. *Key concept:* situation selection

- **A**lter your attention. *Key concept:* distraction

- **R**eframe the situation. *Key concept:* reappraisal

- **T**ag your emotions. *Key concept:* labeling

- **S**tep back. *Key concept:* self-distancing

Change Your Circumstances through Situation Selection/Modification

This concept is the most forward thinking of all the CARTS concepts and probably the simplest to do. For example, think about public speaking. Surveys reveal that the number one fear in America is the fear of public speaking. Let's assume you're a small-business owner and you've been asked to bring a speech to the local Rotary club about your business. After you read the invitation, you got a knot in your stomach and a headache. Speaking has never been your strength. The more you think about it, the more you dread it. You could modify the circumstance by simply refusing to go. But in doing so, you will lose the opportunity to grow and to tell prospective clients about your company. If you decline, you've dealt with your fears by not putting yourself in the situation. But, you've also lost out on potential new business.

The Bible shows us that not putting yourself in such a situation may be the wisest choice. Jesus once healed a man whose hand was shriveled. Because it was the Sabbath, the Pharisees got angry with him and began to plot how they could kill him. The scripture says that Jesus withdrew from that place (Matt 15). He knew what they were up to and changed his circumstances (withdrew) to avoid having to deal with them because God's timetable for his final days had not yet arrived. He made the right choice to not put himself in harm's way. Other times he walked right into it. Proverbs 27:12 also tells us that smart people will alter their circumstances by wisely avoiding some situations: "Prudent people see evil and hide; the simpleminded go right to it and get punished."

In the case of the speaker, you could still accept the invitation and apply this concept by arriving early and making yourself more familiar with the speaking venue. Although you're not physically changing anything, by becoming more familiar with the space, in a sense you're altering it in your mind by changing how you perceive it. By doing so, you can lower your threat level and thereby moderate your fear. You could also make a change in the room by asking the host to reposition the lectern so you could feel more comfortable.

Alter Your Attention through Distraction

Alter your attention through distraction means to shift your attention away from what's bothering you. It's often helpful in the short term. Young parents with small children do this all the time in church if their child gets fussy. They'll pull out keys, toys, or crayons to distract their children from whatever is making them restless. This same principle applies here, only we distract *ourselves* from the emotion-causing situation.

Let's revisit our speaker illustration again. Assume you've accepted the invitation to speak, and as you pull into the parking lot, fear starts to grow. What can you do? Here are some distraction ideas. Before you get up to speak, you could distract yourself by checking some of the latest sports scores on your iPhone—discreetly, of course. When you get up to speak, instead of looking at disinterested, frowning faces, focus on two or three positive and affirming ones. I've had to use this simple technique several times when I've spoken.

In every church I've led, there were always a few passive-aggressive people who showed their mean side when I preached. I recall how one man who didn't like me would dramatically flip through the pages of the Bible as I spoke, showing his disdain for me and my teaching. You could hear the page turn's *swoosh* reverberate in the auditorium. If I focused on him, I'd get angry, which would suck the mental resources from my *CEO* that I needed to be at my best. However, when I scanned the audience and focused on affirming faces, my anger subsided and I felt more confident while I preached.

In Jesus's most famous sermon, the Sermon on the Mount, he taught about worry. Many of Jesus's followers were very poor, so they often worried about food and clothing. While not minimizing their real needs, Jesus explained the futility of worry and that if they put God first, God promised to take care of them. In the following passage in Matthew 6, he modeled distraction as a way to quiet anxious emotions, at least for a time. He pointed to two common images from nature, birds and flowers, perhaps even pointing to them as he preached. This act illustrates how he diverted the attention of his listeners.

> Therefore, I say to you, don't worry about your life, what you'll eat or what you'll drink, or about your body, what you'll wear. Isn't life more than food and the body more than clothes? *Look at the birds in the sky.* They don't sow seed or harvest grain or gather crops into barns. Yet your heavenly Father feeds them. Aren't you worth much more than they are? Who among you by worrying can add a single moment to your life? And why do you worry about clothes? *Notice how the lilies in the field grow.* They don't wear themselves out with work, and they don't spin cloth. But I say to you that even Solomon in all of his splendor wasn't dressed like one of these. If God dresses grass in the field so beautifully, even though it's alive today and tomorrow it's thrown into the furnace, won't God do much more for you, you people of weak faith? (Matt 6:25-30, emphasis added)

Although modifying your circumstances and altering your attention can help you control your emotions in the short term, the next three concepts provide longer-term benefit.

I use the metaphor of a teeter-totter for the concepts that follow. As I described earlier, as I processed my pain with my decision to leave my church, some days felt like a teeter-totter. I'd seem to do well for a while, then an hour or so later not so well. I learned that for each of these concepts, there is an opposite, like the opposite side of a teeter-totter. I contrast both sides in each of the next three and suggest a counterbalance for each one that can help strengthen the helpful practices over against the unhelpful responses. Here they are:

- *Reappraisal* (viewing the issue differently) versus rumination (wallowing in my negative emotions)

- *Counterbalance:* a coach
- *Labeling* (naming my emotion) versus suppression (stuffing my emotion)
    - *Counterbalance:* journaling
- *Distancing* (seeing the situation as if you are a third person) versus immersion (reliving the situation over and over) (Kross & Ayduk, 2008)
    - *Counterbalance:* a camera viewfinder metaphor

Reframe the Situation through Reappraisal

As I processed the shock of my transition that I mentioned earlier, I tended to wallow in negative thinking. I genuinely wanted to learn from my experience, and if I simply expunged it from my mind (even if I could), I wouldn't grow to become a better leader. Yet when I thought about what had happened, I easily became depressed. I was doing something called rumination, revisiting and rehashing my situation and emotions. Rumination is closely linked to depression and anxiety and reactivates the emotions that caused our distress in the first place (Nolen-Hoeksema et al., 2008). I felt stuck and hopeless as I ruminated and mulled over my pain.

Rumination was keeping me from learning helpful lessons from my experience. And if I didn't grow in my self-leadership through this, it could hinder my future leadership in another church. A leader's self-leadership, whether good or bad, can profoundly impact the organization he or she leads (Manz, 1986). I needed something or someone to help me pull out of my mire of negativity.

In my case, distraction only helped for short bits of time. I could watch a TV program that might get my mind off my pain, but my brain would remember it once the program was over. Fortunately, I began to learn about other emotional regulation techniques, of which reappraisal (reframing a situation) was one. Researchers have discovered that reappraisal depresses activity in our *Panic Alarm* and activates our *CEO* (Goldin et al., 2008).

Reframing the situation through reappraisal is choosing to see the situation in a different way, seeing life from God's perspective. Although it takes practice to maximize reframing, this option quiets our *Panic Alarm* longer than does distraction. This concept works best when we've actually begun to feel an emotion and distraction hasn't helped. It's also best to do when we can get into a calm setting rather than when we are in the heat of an emotional setting. When we reframe or reappraise a situation, we think about it in a different way so that it doesn't distress us as much. When we think those positive thoughts, our brain's *Rewarder-Motivator* also gets activated (Layous et al., 2011).

Chapter 8 explains team collaboration from a brain-based perspective. There I will unpack a concept called certainty, but I'll touch on it here. The brain loves certainty about the future. Because the brain is like a prediction machine, certainty gives it clarity and a sense of what's coming next (Rock & Cox, 2012). And reappraisal helps create more certainty in our minds and can thus calm anxious emotions.

We can reappraise in several ways. We can normalize a situation by telling ourselves, "If someone were in my shoes, they'd probably feel the same way about the situation that I do." In my case, most pastors experiencing what I did would probably feel similar feelings. That simple thought helped me realize that I wasn't a weak leader for feeling as I did. Another way to reappraise is to put ourselves in their shoes, which helps us gain a different perspective. This perspective, seeing the other person's side, helps calm our *Panic Alarm* when we're in conflict. I did this several times by mentally putting myself in the shoes of one leader with whom I often faced conflict, to see his perspective. When I did, I calmed down.

A third way is to decide that a situation you perceived threatens you simply doesn't anymore. It's putting it into perspective. Reappraisal began to help me realize that the intensity of my transition was diminishing and I could now see it as part of God's plan. In one study researchers showed participants, in an fMRI, pictures of people standing outside a church, crying. They assumed it was a funeral. The researchers then told them to imagine it was a wedding. Immediately the researchers noticed a decrease in activation in the brain's *Panic Alarm* and an increase in activation in their *Impulse Brake* (McRae, 2011). When we reappraise, we gain more emotional control.

Another way we can reappraise is to consider the placebo effect. Years ago when a doctor felt that a person's medical problem was "in his head" he could prescribe a pill that he told the patient would help him. However, it was nothing more than a sugar pill. Anecdotally, many of those patients improved. Due to ethics issues today, doctors can't do that except in trials. When the neurosurgeon implanted the device in Tiffany's brain that I described in chapter 1, we didn't know for three months if it was turned on. The reason? The neurologist had to account for the "placebo effect."

Now that we can peer into the brain, studies have shown that the placebo effect actually improves health, specifically by moderating depression (Mayberg et al., 2002). So reappraising the future with optimism (i.e., this pill will help me or tomorrow will be a better day) can help quiet the amygdala in our *Panic Alarm*, even though we may have no guarantee about the future (Sharot et al., 2007). And studies show that in general those who reappraise experience more positive emotions, simply feel better overall, and get along better with others (Gross & John, 2003).

For the Christian, Philippians 4:8 reflects this optimism: "From now on, brothers and sisters, if anything is excellent and if anything is admirable, focus your thoughts on these things: all that is true, all that is holy, all that is just, all that is pure, all that is lovely, and all that is worthy of praise." This verse tells us to reappraise, to direct our thinking in a more positive direction. When we think more positively (for a Christian, thinking in biblical ways), researchers have discovered that we actually feel better because positive thinking increases one of the feel-good neurotransmitters, dopamine (Goldin et al., 2008). Scripture also reminds us to reframe our sufferings by putting them into a larger context: "Instead, rejoice as you share Christ's suffering. You share his suffering now so that you may also have overwhelming joy when *his glory is revealed*" (1 Pet 4:13, emphasis added).

Although reappraisal helped, I didn't seem to have the mental strength to reappraise for long periods of time. Rumination would often smother the potential benefits reappraisal offered. I realized I needed help.

David Rock and Ann Betz, an experienced coach who incorporates neuroscience into her coaching practice, have both discovered that reappraisal happens best with the help of a coach (Rock & Cox, 2012, and Betz, 2011). So I sought out a coach. In fact, I worked with two coaches for a time. I was amazed at how their counsel and fresh eyes helped me objectively reframe my situation. As a result, my negative thinking intruded into my thoughts less often. I began to see that leaving the church, as difficult as it was with no certain future, could open up new opportunities for me. My coaches gave me the extra mental leverage to counterbalance my tendency to ruminate.

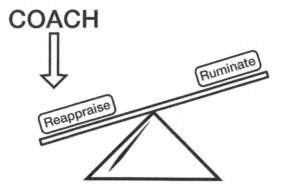

Tag Your Emotions through Labeling

Another brain-based concept that helped me manage my emotions is *tagging your emotions through labeling*. In my church experience, my emotions weren't pleasant, so it seemed natural to suppress them. For most of my adult life I responded to painful emotions with a *grin-and-bear-it*, a *grown-men-don't-cry*, or a *put-on-the-poker-face* response. In fact, one study showed that one-third of all our lies are about how we feel (DePaulo et al., 1996).

Unfortunately, in my years as a pastor, I've seen many leaders, especially men, buy into this so-called "manly" way to deal with our painful emotions. The only problem is that it just doesn't work and actually works against us (Richards & Gross, 2006). Neuroscientists have found that stuffing, denying, or ignoring our emotions reinforces them (Roemer & Borkovec, 1994), affects short-term memory, increases blood pressure, and robs our brain's *CEO* of the mental energy it needs (Richards & Gross, 2006, and Gross, 2002). It's like trying to consciously quit thinking about a purple giraffe. The more we try to quit thinking about it, the stronger the image gets.

If a conversation with someone causes emotions to spike, and we try to stuff them, it dampens our ability to listen to that person. Because we pay more attention to the emotion than to the conversation, we miss important information from the interaction. Although we can't stop the feeling of an emotion, we can control how we express it with our actions. Ephesians 4:26 reminds us of this when it states, "*Be angry without sinning. Don't let the sun set on your anger.*" We can feel anger yet respond to it in a God-honoring way.

Although it may seem counterintuitive, tagging your emotions, through labeling and naming them by putting feelings into words, actually recruits our *Impulse Brake* and dampens activity in our *Panic Alarm* (Lieberman et al.,

2007). We label them when we acknowledge them to ourselves and, when appropriate, to others. If you feel angry in a staff meeting, mentally admit to yourself that you're angry. Or you may ask for a break in the meeting so you can be alone a few minutes to verbally admit, "Lord, I'm struggling with anger right now. Please help me calm my emotions so I can be at my best in this meeting." In fact, labeling may actually help men more than women because men don't talk as much about their feelings as women do. So when men do this, it's a novel experience, and the brain likes novelty. Also, children taught to label their emotions even perform better in school and experience better relationships (Gottman et al., 1975).

In my case, I began to label my emotions. When I felt anger, I called it anger. When I felt sad, I admitted my sadness. Audibly naming those emotions helped arrest the emotion's intensity and thus my tendency to become negative. However, journaling, another tangible way to label emotions, helped me apply this concept most effectively.

In one study researchers asked participants to write for eighty minutes. They asked one group to write about a negative emotional event in their lives and the other group was asked to write about anything nonemotional. They tracked the participants and found that one year later those who wrote about the negative event had fewer reasons to go to the doctor. Apparently the act of writing about their negative emotions and labeling them improved their physical and emotional health (Baikie & Wilhelm, 2005).

Journaling provided a useful counterbalance that helped tip my response from suppressing my emotions to labeling them, as the following diagram illustrates. My tendency toward negativity didn't fully dissipate, but journaling about my experience took the sting and power out of the negative emotions. And the more I practiced labeling through journaling, the more habitual and helpful this tool became.

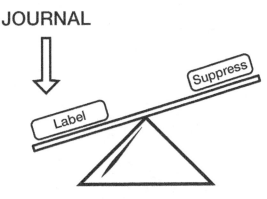

I believe Peter's admonition in 1 Peter 5:7 to "throw all your anxiety onto him, because he cares about you" describes this concept in action. To *cast our anxiety* implies we must admit that we feel anxious and call it what it is. Also King David in the Psalms often illustrates this concept when he repeatedly verbalizes his painful emotions. Jeremiah also represents this, as he was even called the weeping prophet.

Step Back through Self-Distancing

The third mental process I used to counter my negativity was *self-distancing, taking a third-person view of an emotional situation* (the proverbial fly on the wall). Dr. Ethan Kross has shown that distancing, versus taking the first-person perspective (immersion), dampens activity in our *Panic Alarm* (Kross & Ayduk, 2008). Of all three of my "teeter-totter self-leadership approaches," this one reduced my emotionality and negativity most often.

When my mind began to wander into negative territory about my experience, I tried to see the bigger picture to discover insights from it by taking on a *distant me* perspective. That is, I chose to *not* relive the experience again as a first person by immersing myself in the meetings and discussions that led to my departure. Instead, I imagined myself observing those meetings and discussions afterwards through the viewfinder of a camera. My viewfinder perspective counterbalanced my self-immersion tendency. Instead of recounting the experience, I tried to reconstrue it and learn from it as I viewed it through my imaginary viewfinder. The following "lens" word picture gave me a way to stay focused on a more positive perspective as that third-person learner.

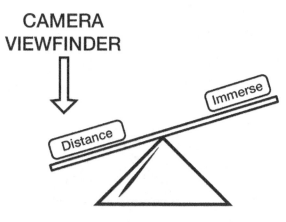

I genuinely wanted to learn from my experience and grow as a leader. By taking this distant third-person perspective, two things happened. First, I thought more clearly because I engaged my brain's *CEO*. This third-person view helped me more objectively own my part of the problem and cast less blame on the other leaders. These men with whom I disagreed were good men. Philosophical differences, not ethical issues in their character or mine, prompted me to step down. I wanted to treat them with the respect and honor they were due, including how I thought about them. Secondly, I was able to quiet my *Panic Alarm*, which in turn helped me stay more positive and less anxious.

As a result, I ruminated less and revisited the negativity of the experience less often. I was able to experience the positive effects from self-distancing that brain researchers have discovered lasts a long time (Kross & Ayduk, 2008). The benefits include decreased emotions, better resolution to our problem, the issue becoming less central in our lives, and decreased intrusive thoughts (distracting, painful thoughts that randomly pop into our minds).

Self-distancing helped me shift from an emotional response that made me negative to a more thoughtful response that prompted a more teachable and positive mind-set. The camera viewfinder gave me an easy-to-remember mental hook that helped counterbalance the temptation to immerse myself in negativity.

In Matthew 11 Jesus denounced places where people had refused to repent. Immediately following this teaching he brings comfort to his followers who faced difficulty with one of the most beautiful promises in scripture.

> Come to me, all you who are struggling hard and carrying heavy loads, and I will give you rest. Put on my yoke, and learn from me. I'm gentle and humble. And you will find rest for yourselves. My yoke is easy to bear, and my burden is light. (Matt 11:28-30)

He's telling us to mentally step back from our personal difficulties to imagine ourselves yoked to Jesus, an image that illustrates self-distancing. His yoke will give us rest as we unyoke ourselves from our hurts and pains. From a different perspective, immersing ourselves in his promises and love is a great way to appropriately use immersion.

Summary and Final Thoughts

In this chapter I covered the first of the four leadership domains, emotional regulation. As a self-leadership competency, it lays the foundation for the other domains. The acronym CARTS described five tools we can use to keep our emotions in check.

Change your circumstances. *Key concept:* situation selection

Alter your attention. *Key concept:* distraction

Reframe the situation. *Key concept:* reappraisal

Important tool: a coach

Tag your emotions. *Key concept:* labeling

Important tool: journaling

Step back. *Key concept:* self-distancing

Important tool: an image of a camera viewfinder

Sometimes, however, we do our very best to keep our emotions in check but simply don't have the reserves to do so. In the short term, when we're hungry or tired, our *CEO* is less likely to override an active *Panic Alarm*. In that case we can usually remedy that with adequate sleep and healthy food to recharge our *CEO*. However, sometimes that doesn't even help and we may even sleep or eat too much to avoid difficult circumstances. When that happens, it's like walking on a sprained ankle. Until it heals, you can easily step the wrong way and feel intense pain. With a normal ankle, it's strong enough to take a twist here and there or a misstep and feel little pain. In a similar way, sometimes we have little emotional reserve and the smallest leadership conflict or disappointment can put our *Panic Alarm* into overdrive.

If that's true for you, you may be chronically stressed. Chronic anxiety and stress cause what scientists call *allostatic load*, a term for wear and tear on the body. Prolonged stress and an unceasing emotional environment create sustained high levels of cortisol, the stress hormone. When our body secretes too much cortisol over long periods of time, these problems can affect us: impaired immunity, weight gain, greater emotional reactivity, heart problems, decreased memory, and diminished brain functioning. If you find yourself in that situation, you probably need a sustained break from your work and some counseling or coaching. You may even realize that you need to find a different job. Don't be afraid to make such a move. Your physical, emotional, and family health matters to God.

As you practice these concepts, they will become second nature. I'm still learning how to use them more consistently myself. Over time, though, as we regularly use them, we'll push them into our brain's *Automatic Transmission* (basal ganglia) and they'll be at our service more quickly without depleting our limited mental resources as they once did.

We experience life and leadership much like a teeter-totter. A good day at work or at home can swing to a bad day. And we often can't control what comes at us. But with the Holy Spirit's help, we can apply neuroscience insight such as situation selection, distraction, reappraisal, labeling, and distancing to help us control our emotions. A coach can help counterbalance rumination through reappraisal. Journaling provides a way to label our emotions and avoid suppressing them. And the mental picture of a camera viewfinder can help us take a third person's perspective so that we can distance ourselves from a painful experience, learn from it, and avoid immersion. An old Chinese proverb captures the gist of emotional regulation: *Anger is the wind that blows out the lamp of the mind.*

In the next chapter we'll look at the next self-leadership domain: personal productivity.

The science behind . . . *Brain Surprise 6*: *If you put a pencil sideways in your mouth and pull your lips back, your brain will make you feel happier.*

In one study when participants did this after a mental challenge and a pain test, they recovered more quickly and showed less stress than participants who did not. Apparently even a fake smile (or even standing straight) can affect the brain's emotional processing and positively affect mood. It's called the facial feedback theory (McGonigal, 2012).

Chapter 7

Brain-Savvy Personal Productivity

Brain Surprise 7: *If you're feeling down, go pet a dog. Your brain just might make you feel better.*

As an engineering student at Georgia Tech, I often attended Atlanta symphony concerts. If Tech students arrived thirty minutes before the concert began and if it weren't sold out, we could get in at a cheap price. Since I enjoy classical music, I often took advantage of the discount. It was also a classy, cheap date if I wanted to impress a girl.

Without exception, when I walked into the symphony hall the music sounded horrible. In fact, it didn't sound like music at all. It sounded like a cacophony where stringed instruments, horns, percussion, and wind instruments seemed to battle against each other. Without any consistent rhythm, structure, or harmony, it was hard on the ears. Of course, this discord was to be expected. Why? Prior to the concert, every player would tune his or her instrument and practice individual parts, with no regard for what the other players played.

Then, exactly at eight o'clock, the concert's start time, the cacophony would cease as the conductor stepped up to the podium. He'd lift his baton and lead the symphony into a rousing rendition of Beethoven's Fifth or some other beautiful composition.

Before the conductor, I experienced cacophony. After the conductor, it was harmony.

95

The pre- and post-conductor image describes what our brains face each day. A cacophony of information bombards us every hour. One author describes this data overload as *infobesity* (Pearrow, 2012). And when data overloads our brain, our *CEO* can shut down. British psychologist Dr. David Lewis coined a term to describe what happens from infobesity as "Information Fatigue Syndrome." Symptoms include burnout, a compulsion to constantly check e-mail or the web, poor concentration, hostility (Elwart, 2013), and anxiety caused by activation of our *Panic Alarm* (Dimoka et al., forthcoming).

It's no wonder that our ability to think gets muddled when we consider the massive amount of information produced every single *minute*. These stats only reflect 2012. And each year data overload continues to grow (Elwart, 2013).

- 72 hours of video posts
- 347 blog posts
- 700,000 Facebook entries
- 30,000 tweets
- 2 million e-mails
- 12 million text messages

So what can we do with this data onslaught to avoid a preconcert-like cacophony in our brains? The answer lies in this chapter on brain-savvy personal productivity. Here I suggest three key ways we can hone our brain's effectiveness for God's glory. Several scriptures speak to the responsibility God gives us to make the most of our life on earth. One way we do that is through stewarding how we care for every part of our being, including our brains.

- "So be careful to live your life wisely, not foolishly. Take advantage of every opportunity because these are evil times." (Eph 5:15-16)

- "Let me know my end, LORD. How many days do I have left? I want to know how brief my time is." (Ps 39:4)

- "Pay attention, you who say, 'Today or tomorrow we will go to such-and-such a town. We will stay there a year, buying and selling, and making a profit.' You don't really know about tomorrow.

What is your life? You are a mist that appears for only a short while before it vanishes. Here's what you ought to say: 'If the Lord wills, we will live and do this or that.' But now you boast and brag, and all such boasting is evil. It is a sin when someone knows the right thing to do and doesn't do it." (Jas 4:13-17)

The metaphor of an oar works to capture three essentials related to self-leadership and productivity. In order to lead others well, we must lead ourselves well. Here's what the acronym OAR represents.

O: Optimization (relates to mental load and brain space)

A: Attention (relates to focus and inhibiting distractions)

R: Reflection (relates to thinking about your thinking through a process called mindfulness)

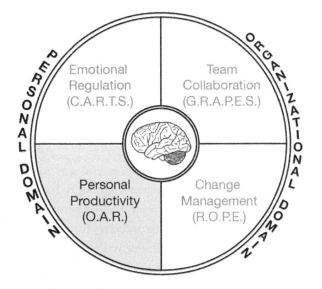

Optimization: Relates to Mental Load and Brain Space

You'll recall that our brain's *CEO* has limited capacity to operate. It's much like the limited drawing space on the old Etch A Sketch toy. It fills up quickly. And it operates in a serial manner, processing one piece of information at a time. When we try to process too much conscious information at once, our *CEO* gets clogged, we think less clearly, and our *Panic Alarm* can easily get activated. As a result, we don't lead as well. As David Rock says, we get too many actors (thoughts) on the stage of our brain (Rock, 2009, p. 20). So what can we do to optimize our brain's space to avoid these bottlenecks? I suggest the following seven habits.

1. Put First Things First

First things first is another way to say prioritize prioritizing. When we seek to put things in the right order of importance, we can keep that bottleneck from occurring in our *CEO*. This is as simple as making a list of what you want to accomplish each day, prioritizing what's most important and what takes the greatest mental focus, and then doing those tasks first.

Prioritizing is an abstract process and takes considerable effort from our *CEO*. It requires comparing items and making a judgment. So it's best to do this when your brain is fresh, usually in the morning before your day begins.

For a Christian, Matthew 6:33 gives us our overarching priority that provides an umbrella under which everything else falls: "Instead, desire first and foremost God's kingdom and God's righteousness, and all these things will be given to you as well."

2. Exercise

Scientists increasingly see exercise as a powerful way to keep your brain healthy. Neuroscientist Dr. John Ratey wrote an entire book on the subject called *Spark: The Revolutionary New Science of Exercise and the Brain*. He explains that exercise increases a key protein necessary for a healthy brain, *BDNF* (brain derived neurotropic factor). Brain derived means that the brain makes it, and neurotropic implies that it helps make neurons strong. It's considered the master molecule of learning (Ratey, 2013, p. 38) that he calls "Miracle-Gro for the brain." This brain fertilizer benefits the brain in many ways. It protects neurons from premature death, improves their function, enhances communication between them, stimulates their growth (neurogenesis), and provides a key link between emotions and thoughts (Ratey, 2013, p. 40).

One study showed that even one thirty-five-minute workout on a treadmill at 60 to 70 percent of maximum heart rate can improve our brain's processing speed and cognitive flexibility (Ratey, 2013, p. 34). Cognitive flexibility is a term that describes your *CEO*'s ability to shift its thinking and to create new ideas. As leaders, this ability is crucial. So, the next time you schedule an important creative meeting, a good workout or a walk prior to it can enhance your creativity.

In one study, neuroscientist Arthur Kramer divided fifty-nine sedentary senior adults into two groups (Ratey, 2013, p. 226). One group simply did stretching exercises for six months while the other group exercised three times a week on a treadmill for six months. MRI scans showed that the frontal and temporal lobes of those who exercised actually increased in volume, a surprising finding. And their brains looked two to three years younger than the brains of the stretch-only group. Other studies have shown similar brain volume increases attributed to exercise (Colcombe et al., 2006).

3. Sleep

Work demands never seem to end. There's always one more report to complete, another sermon to preach, another call to make, and more e-mails to answer. Often we cut back on sleep to squeeze more time to accomplish more, thinking we'll get more done. So many people have cut back on their sleep that sleep deprivation is now a national epidemic. In 2008 the Centers for Disease Control and Prevention discovered that over 35 percent of adults age twenty-five to sixty-five report that during the past month they unintentionally fell asleep. Five percent said that they fell asleep at the wheel. And 35 percent got fewer than seven hours of sleep a night (CDC, 2013), even though many experts agree that most adults need seven to nine hours each night (National Sleep Foundation, n.d.). And the effects of sleep deprivation in the United States cost businesses more than $100 billion per year (Medina, 2009, p. 165).

Getting less sleep does NOT help us become more productive. In addition to feeling sluggish and cranky, researchers have discovered several other negative impacts to our brain (Sousa, 2012, p. 114) that include these:

- Decreased attention, alertness, and cognitive response speed.
  One study showed that the cognitive ability loss from sleeping
  fewer than six hours a night for just five nights matched the loss a
  person experienced who hadn't slept for forty-eight hours straight
  (Dinges et al., 1997).

- Dampened creativity.

- Impaired function of our mirror neurons, our *CEO* (prefrontal cortex), our *Error Detector* (anterior cingulate cortex), and our *Rememberer* (hippocampus).

When we don't get enough sleep, we rob our brains of important neural functions because the brain is actually very active during sleep. Although the brain never really shuts down, it's only truly at rest during non-REM sleep, which accounts for only 20 percent of our normal sleep cycle. During the other 80 percent, sleep helps the brain encode, strengthen, stabilize, and consolidate our memories from the day. Our brain's *Accountant* replays what we have learned during the day (Medina, 2009, p. 164) to make our memories stick. Sleep also plays an important role in learning and problem solving.

Are you sleep deprived? Take this quiz. If you answer yes to more than two, you probably need more sleep.

- After I get up, I feel tired most of the day.

- I often hit the snooze button in the morning.

- I wake up a lot at night.

- I often feel mentally sluggish during the day.

- On weekends and vacations I sleep a lot longer than I normally do to "catch up."

- I tend to load up on caffeine through coffee, energy drinks, or sodas to "keep me going."

- Within a couple of hours of going to bed, I exercise or spend a lot of time in front of my computer monitor or my tablet computer.

Here are a few tips to consider if you need more sleep.

1. Realize that sleep and rest are biblical. We see this in the creation account and God's establishing sabbath rest as a principle. We see this in Jesus telling his disciples to pull away from the demands of

ministry and rest (Matt 6:31). And we see Jesus sleeping, even in a storm (Matt 4:38).

2. Consider taking a power nap. You'll be in good company because Einstein, Napoleon, and Beethoven took daytime naps.

3. Go to bed thirty minutes earlier each night. It's usually easier to do that than to sleep later.

4. Limit evening meetings.

4. Simplify the Complex

When ideas or concepts get too complex, they take up too much brain space. As a result they crowd out our ability for other important brain tasks, like perspective taking, defining reality, and attention.

If you've ever heard a speaker constantly use complex terms you didn't understand, your brain space likely got bottlenecked. You probably missed much of what he said by trying to make mental connections to his complex ideas. On the other hand, if you've heard a speaker describe the complex with simple terms, your brain used its space more effectively and you probably learned more.

While in college I tried three times to complete an engineering course in dynamics, a branch of physics that studies forces and their effect on motion. I dropped the course twice because those two professors spoke way over my head. However, the third time I took the course I earned an A. Why? The professor simplified the content so that my brain was able to comprehend it. He didn't skip anything nor did he dumb things down. He just simplified things.

So the next time you tackle some difficult topic or project, break it down into smaller, bite-sized, more easily understood pieces. In doing so you'll use your brain space more effectively. And when you prepare a sermon or Bible study, keep simplicity in mind for the benefit of your audience.

5. Group Similar Information through Chunking

Dr. George Miller (1920–2012), one of the founders of cognitive psychology, is most known for his oft-cited paper, "The Magical Number Seven, Plus or Minus Two" (Vitello, 2012). In this paper he proposed that the working memory in our *CEO* can hold seven items at once, plus or minus two, now known as *Miller's law*. Since then some scientists have narrowed down what we can hold in our working memory to three or four items (Kane & Engle, 2003). So when we reach our limits, we need to do something with that extra information. Chunking helps.

Chunking means grouping or categorizing similar items together in our memory or on paper. It helps improve our working memory's capacity. Chess masters become masters not because they memorize every possible move, but because they chunk individual moves into categories that they access depending on their opponents' moves (Groot, 1965). To see how this works, try this chunking exercise. Get a pencil and paper and look at this nine-digit number for five seconds and try to memorize it. Then look away and write down what you recall.

752390459

How did you do? You probably left out a number or two because your *CEO* ran out of space. Now try the same thing with this number by memorizing this nine-digit number as three, three-digit numbers.

615 274 852

How did you do this time? You probably recalled these three, three-digit numbers more accurately than the nine-digit number.

This book uses this technique in presenting the four leadership domains by coupling each with a visual metaphor: carts, oar, grapes, and rope. Each metaphor evokes an image. Each letter in the spelling of each word represents a word or a phrase that describes a way to develop that domain in your leadership. You more likely can recall the specifics when your brain first remembers the image, then the letters in the image's word, and then the corresponding phrase or word. I could have simply listed the concepts without chunking, but your recall probably would have suffered.

Chunking can help you plan projects when you clump similar tasks together. It can also boost your time management if you chunk similar tasks together and then do them at the same time (i.e., answer e-mail twice a day instead of every ten minutes).

I mention the final two habits only briefly.

6. Automate

You'll recall that our *Automatic Transmission* (basil ganglia) is where our brain stores habits. We don't need to use precious mental energy to perform a habit. We do it "without thinking." So, the more habits you can create (the more you automate what you do), the more brain space you'll have available for other tasks.

7. Motivate Yourself with Small Wins

When we accomplish goals, even small ones, our brain secretes dopamine, which feels good because it activates our *Rewarder-Motivator* (nucleus accumbens). During the day if you feel unmotivated, find a small goal and accomplish it. You'll get a small boost of dopamine to help you feel more motivated. Simply checking something off your to-do list can help optimize your brain's resources by not only rewarding you but by preventing you from thinking about it in the background and thus using up limited brain resources.

Attention: Relates to Focus and Inhibiting Distraction

Our brains get easily distracted. As I write this paragraph in a Panera Bread restaurant, I'm struggling to block out these mental distractions: the voices of two women chatting at the table next to me, my temptation to check the status of an audiobook downloading on my iPhone, and my internal dialogue debating whether or not to refill my Diet Pepsi. It takes a lot of effort to pay attention, especially in today's data-rich environment.

Constant chatter from our cell phones, computers, and other high-tech devices tempts us to distraction. In fact, psychologists have described this problem caused with the term ADT for *Attention Deficit Trait* (Gilbert, 2005). ADT has afflicted as many as 30 to 40 percent of the workforce. It results in hurry, diminished creativity, reduced productivity, sleeplessness, and putting in more hours while getting less done. And work interruptions can diminish our attention by causing us to take up to 50 percent longer on a task, resulting in 50 percent more errors (CubeSmart, 2002). Although akin to ADHD, ADT goes away when we go on vacation because work chatter usually decreases.

Linda Stone, a former VP at Microsoft, captured our attention problem with the term *continuous partial attention* (Stone, n.d.). She describes it this way: "To pay continuous partial attention is to keep a top-level item in focus, and constantly scan the periphery in case something more important emerges." As a result, this always-on mode puts our brain on constant alert, thus flooding it with too much stress hormone that in turn slows our brain's processing speed.

So what can we do to quell this chatter? The first concept in OAR focused on optimizing your brain space, strengthening and freeing it up so that you can focus on the next concept, represented by the letter "A." "A" stands for attention, focusing on what we must while at the same time inhibiting distractions.

It's helpful to first understand what happens in the brain during attention and distraction. Three concepts help explain this.

The Inverted "U"'

For your *CEO* to work most effectively, the environment has to be just right, much like Goldilocks in the fairy tale where everything had to be "just right." Neurotransmitters play a vital role in this "just right" state. Amy Arnsten, one of the leading researchers on attention, uses an inverted "U" to describe how specific neurotransmitters (especially dopamine and norepinephrine) affect the *CEO* (see the following figure; Brennan & Arnsten, 2008). With too few neurotransmitters in our *CEO*, the left side of the inverted "U," we can get easily distracted, disorganized, forgetful, and disinhibited. This can happen when we feel unmotivated, tired, or bored.

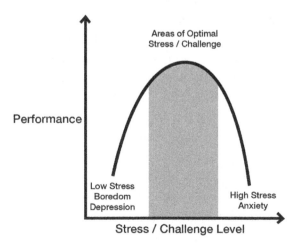

On the right side of the inverted "U," when we get too many neuro-transmitters in our brain, we get stressed and anxious. However, if they're balanced at the top of the inverted "U," we're focused, organized, and responsible. Coffee, caffeinated drinks (but not too many), exercise, and novelty can increase the amount of these neurotransmitters and get us into a more productive and focused state. The optimal environment also depends on the task we're doing.

Synchrony

Another way to understand attention is to see the brain as the symphony orchestra illustration I used in the beginning of the chapter. Our *CEO* is like the brain's conductor that helps focus our attention through synchronizing the brain's processes. If fact, when we focus, a brain wave called the gamma band, our fastest brain wave, sweeps across our brain forty times a second to bring all the brain's "instruments" together to form the "symphony" of attention. It's called synchrony. This process binds the various brain regions together to aid learning and enhance attention. This is Hebb's law in action. *Brain cells that fire together wire together.*

Attentional Networks

A third concept about attention comes from Michael Posner, a scientist who three decades ago developed a paradigm about how our brain pays attention. This still-popular model describes attention with three distinct brain processes or networks.

AROUSE → ATTEND → ACT

In the *arouse* phase, since our brain is always scanning our environment for something unusual, when something unexpected happens, it senses it and is alerted. Norepinephrine enhances these signals. In the *attend* phase, we orient our attention to it to get more information. Acetylcholine, another neuro-transmitter important for learning, plays a role in this phase. And in the *act* phase, we do something in response to the stimulus. Dopamine plays a role here as it blocks other distractions. We might think of this process as the three parts of firing a gun. We load it. We aim it. And then we fire it. People with

ADHD experience a breakdown in these processes. They suffer an imbalance in these chemicals, which causes them to often choose immediate gratification over their current goals.

For example, as I write this section, again in Panera (my favorite place to write in the United States), I'm sitting in a corner booth with my face to the wall. I'm trying to concentrate with the help of an energy drink (caffeine helps boost dopamine) and my sound-suppressing headphones, which dampen the conversations around me. Immediately behind me sit three high school girls studying together. Occasionally I hear sounds loud enough that filter into my ears even past my headphones. My *alerting* system has activated. A few times I've slowed my typing a bit and become aware that it's the girls. My *attending* system was activated at that point. Then my *acting* system decides what to do. I will either pay attention to what they are saying, refocus on my writing, or take a break to give my brain a rest. However, the more engaged and interested I am in my writing at that moment, the more focused I am upon it and the better I'm able to inhibit the noisy distractions.

Several of my brain's players played a role in this scenario when I stayed focused on my current goal to write this chapter. Although an fMRI was not monitoring my brain in Panera, these brain players generally get activated in the attentional process.

My *Error Detector* (anterior cingulate cortex) monitored if my turning to listen to the girls' conversation fit with my current goal, writing this chapter. When it realized that it would add nothing to my goal, it alerted the *CEO* (prefrontal cortex) to intervene, which in turn recruited my *Impulse Brake* (ventral lateral prefrontal cortex) to help me resist the temptation to yield to the distraction. As I've mentioned before, I'm being very simplistic as I describe these processes.

This attention-distraction process goes on in our minds incessantly. And the more often we get distracted, the less productive we become because after each distraction we must reengage our mind and go through the same process once again. The result? The proverbial "Where was I now?" which takes time to reengage our brains in the task. I talk more about how to become aware of this tendency to distraction in the "R" of OAR in the pages ahead.

Before I suggest ways to increase attention, it's also important to realize that we pay closer attention to and remember events that are tied to emotions. Like a chemical Post-it note John Medina describes in his book, *Brain Rules* (Medina, 2009, p. 80), our *Panic Alarm* attaches dopamine to the memory of an emotional stimulus. In addition to our emotions playing a role in attention, familiarity with the potential distraction, our mood at the time, and our memories also affect attention.

Here are three ways to increase your attention.

1. Increase Interest

In the inverted "U" concept I mentioned earlier, I wrote that a lack of dopamine and norepinephrine makes us feel bored and easily distracted. Dopamine helps block out mental noise that can distract our minds, and norepinephrine helps boost our brains' signals to help us maintain attention (Brennan & Arnsten, 2008). One way to boost those chemicals is through finding ways to stay interested in your work.

Have you noticed that time flies when you're interested in something and that it seems to stand still when you're bored? When I was a kid, my mother would cut my hair to save money. I still remember those haircuts in our basement as I sat on a plastic-covered red stool with black legs. I fidgeted the entire time. It took her three hours and forty-two minutes to cut my hair. Well, maybe not that long. Yet when I hunted tadpoles in the pond near our house, it would seem as if I was there only fifteen minutes, although I had begun my hunt three hours earlier.

Did time truly speed up or slow down during those two distinct experiences? Of course not. But when I was focused and attentive on something I liked or that was novel, time seemed to move faster and I paid more attention. Novelty and interest boost the neurotransmitter dopamine and send it to our *Rewarder-Motivator*. It feels good and, well, rewarding. And what gets rewarded we repeat because dopamine also motivates us to want more of a rewarding experience. So when you do something novel or interesting at work or when you study, it can help inhibit distractions and increase attention.

2. Take Brain Breaks

Our brain can only sustain attention for so long before it takes its own break. If you've ever studied for several hours straight or planned a talk or sermon that required intense concentration, you probably found that after one to two hours you got more easily distracted. So in order to sustain attention, build breaks into your routine to refresh your brain so it can continue to maintain attention. Our brains can't stay focused on the same thing for extended periods of time. When we try to push it, we get diminishing returns for our effort.

3. Avoid Multitasking

Many leaders have convinced themselves that multitasking leads to greater productivity. However, researchers have shown that when we try to process two mental tasks at once, our mental capacity can drop from that of a Harvard MBA to that of an eight-year-old. And it can reduce our mental capacities as if we missed a night's sleep or smoked pot (Rock, 2009, pp. 34–36). Multitasking can also diminish long-term memory (Foerde et al., 2006). Even college students who multitasked with their laptops while in a class scored lower on tests than did students who didn't multitask. And students who could see others multitasking also scored lower. So multitasking decreases others' productivity as well as our own (Sana et al., 2013).

When I use the term *multitask*, I don't mean that we can't actually do two things at once. I mean that we can't do two things simultaneously that require our focused *attention*. We can do two things like drive a car and talk to our kids in the backseat because driving takes no conscious effort. It has become deeply ingrained as a habit in our *Automatic Transmission* (basal ganglia).

I purposefully tried one time to prove this concept wrong when two webinars I wanted to watch were scheduled at the same time. I watched one on my computer with the sound on and just listened to the other on my phone. I quickly realized that I couldn't process both webinars at once. I found myself focusing on the computer webinar because it moved at a faster pace and included the visual component. The only way I could focus on the audio portion of the other webinar was to turn my head from my computer monitor and turn off the sound. Each time I switched my attention, though my brain had to reorient and literally "start over" for me to refocus (the attentional network process mentioned earlier repeating itself: arouse-attend-act). Essentially I missed 80 percent of the tele-webinar's material and probably missed 50 percent of the computer webinar's material. And I exhausted my brain trying to pay attention to both. This loss is called "dual-task switch cost." I never really multitasked. I just switched from one webinar to the other. And it kept me from getting much out of either.

Another glaring example of diminished cognitive capacity is talking on a cell phone while driving. Although our driving skills are embedded as habits, neuroscientists have discovered that we impair our thinking ability while talking on a cell phone to the same degree as if we were drunk (Ross & Markman, 1990, pp. 29–58).

Reducing your multitasking tendency will benefit you in many ways. Peter Bregman, author of *18 Minutes: Find Your Focus, Master Distraction, and Get the Right Things Done* and adviser to CEOs, decided to abandon all multitasking for a week. He would only interact with one technology at a time. After his experience, he discovered these benefits (Bregman, 2010).

1. He enjoyed it and found more time with his family.

2. On challenging projects, he made significant progress.

3. His stress dramatically dropped.

4. He became less tolerant of wasted time.

5. His patience for what he enjoyed most and what he found most useful increased.

6. He saw no downside to it.

Here are some tips to reduce tendencies to multitask:

- Set up rules in your meetings about how technology can be used (e.g., no e-mailing and texting except at agreed-upon times when everybody does it).

- Turn off notifications on your computer or mobile device.

- Determine when you will attend to those tasks that interrupted you. When I write or study, I turn off e-mail. But every hour or so when I take a break, I will turn it on and quickly look at e-mail and respond to those that I can at that moment. This allows me to focus on what requires my mental energy and check off those less demanding tasks during those scheduled times.

Reflection: Relates to Mindful Awareness/Thinking about What You Are Thinking About

Our minds are easily distracted. They operate in one of two modes, or networks, the default mode and the direct mode. When our thinking is in the default mode, our minds wander and we lose attention to the task at hand, thoughts just pop into our minds, we can zone out, we become self-absorbed, and we daydream. When in this mode we often become more focused on what's bothering us because our *Error Detector* is activated. External and internal distractions can put us into the default network.

One novel study sought to discover the effects of a wandering mind (Castro, 2010). These researchers developed an iPhone app that made it cost-effective to perform "experience sampling," a technique used to contact people in their daily routine to capture their thoughts, actions, and feelings in the moment. The app would contact the participants (over five thousand) at random moments throughout the day and query them on their activity and happiness. From this group they analyzed 2,250 adults who answered three questions, one each about their self-reported happiness at the moment, their activity at the moment, and whether or not their minds were wandering. Their study revealed these fascinating findings:

- 47 percent were mind wandering at the moment they were asked.

- They were less happy when their minds wandered.

- What they were thinking about more accurately predicted their happiness than what they were doing.

The study concluded with this statement: "A human mind is a wandering mind, and a wandering mind is an unhappy mind. The ability to think about what is not happening is a cognitive achievement that comes at an emotional cost." Of course we can't say that all mind wandering is bad. But their study does point to our need to avoid incessant mind wandering.

Since our brains process and remember bad events more thoroughly than good ones, reflected in one significant research paper as *bad is stronger than good* (Baumeister et al., 2001), it's vital that we develop the discipline of being aware of our thoughts. For if our thoughts often dip into negative thinking, our productivity and attitudes will also dip.

Thinking about our thinking is called "metacognition." The letter "R" in OAR, *reflection*, captures how we do this through a spiritual practice called mindfulness. Practicing mindfulness can help us catch the inner chatter of worry, fear, and anxiety that can throw us into a stress response and hinder our productivity. Mindfulness helps us reclaim our brain space so that our thoughts focus on that which God wants us to focus, instead of worry, about which Jesus preached in Matthew 6.

William James, a brilliant thinker in the late 1890s, is considered to be the father of modern psychology. In his 1,200-page masterwork, *The Principles of Psychology*, he wrote this statement that captures the essence of mindfulness: "The faculty of voluntarily bringing back a wandering attention over and over again, is the very root of judgment, character, and will. No one is *compus sue* (master of self) if he have it not. An education which should improve this faculty would be the education par excellence" (chap. 11).

David Rock explains that mindfulness has pervaded much of our world.

Today, some people refer to the experience of observing yourself as self-awareness or mindfulness. Sometimes it is called metacognition, which means "thinking about your thinking." Or meta-awareness, which means "awareness of your awareness." Whatever it's called, this phenomenon is a central thread in much of the world's literature, appearing as a core idea in philosophy, psychology, ethics, leadership, management, education, learning, training, parenting, dieting, sports, and self-improvement. It's hard to read anything about human experience without someone saying that "knowing yourself" is the first step toward any kind of change. (Rock, 2009, p. 88)

So, mindfulness is less about not getting distracted than it is about engagement, awareness of the present moment. It's a practice than helps us live fully in the present rather than being crucified between the disappointments in the past and the uncertainties of the future. Mindfulness helps us disengage from automatic thoughts, feelings, memories, and reactions. It heightens our self-awareness in real time so that we can accept what we see and experience it in the moment.

Akin to biblical meditation, mindfulness is a spiritual discipline modeled by Brother Lawrence (1640–1691), a monk who lived in a Carmelite monastery in Paris. Although racked with pain from a war injury, he learned to constantly be mindful of the Lord as he washed dishes in the monastery's kitchen. His simple message was this: practice the presence of God. Three hundred years later his letters and conversations were compiled into the book *The Practice of the Presence of God*. Here is one of his insights:

> You are not the only one who is troubled with wandering thoughts. Our mind is extremely roving. But the will is mistress of all of all our faculties. She must recall our stray thoughts and carry them to God as their final end. If the mind is not sufficiently controlled and disciplined at our first engaging in devotion, it contracts certain bad habits of wandering and dissipation.... One way to re-collect the mind easily in the time of prayer, and preserve it more in tranquility, is not to let it wander too far at other times. Keep your mind strictly in the presence of God. (Lawrence, 2011, Kindle e-book loc. 469)

Brother Lawrence sums up the goal for Christian mindfulness: "Above all, get in the habit of often thinking of God, and forget him the least you can" (Lawrence, 2011, Kindle e-book loc. 546).

Learning and practicing mindfulness benefits us in several ways.

- It can help grow new brain cells, neurogenesis (Hölzel et al., 2011).

- It helps ease mild depression, improves emotional regulation, enhances working memory, reduces fatigue, and helps us stay in a better mood (Zeidan et al., 2010).

- It may even have positive benefits on aging by protecting the decline in our brain functions as we get older (Pagnoni & Cekic, 2007).

- It helps us recover more quickly when we get sick (Brown & Ryan, 2003).

- It can help us silence the distracting brain chatter that often overtakes our thinking without our being aware.

- It puts space between an emotional impulse and a behavioral response so that we react less. It helps us stay *in* the moment rather than do something in response *to* the moment.

- It helps us focus more on the Lord and others rather than on ourselves.

- It helps us not only notice emotions and thoughts but also realize that those thoughts and emotions are not us. Mindfulness helps us *describe* our emotions and thoughts rather than instantly *ascribing* some value to them.

Although the word "mindfulness" as a productivity discipline does not appear in the Bible, several scriptures illustrate the concept. But it is important to understand how Christian mindfulness differs from Buddhist mindfulness. Through mindfulness Buddhists strive to empty their minds to reach Nirvana, a so-called state where they vanquish all desire. For a Christian, however, mindfulness helps us declutter our minds of the superfluous so that we desire God more in our daily lives. Spirit-directed mindfulness guides our minds to focus on God's truth about our relationship with him and truth about our current circumstances. Christian mindfulness helps renew our minds, not empty them. These scriptures illustrate the concept of Christian mindfulness.

- In Psalm 37:7 and Psalm 46:10 the psalmist tells us to be still. Mindfulness helps us to mentally and physically still our hearts and bodies before the Lord.

- In multiple places the psalmists meditate on God's words and works, which is a powerful way believers can be fully present for God. The ancient church fathers and mothers often practiced meditation when they separated themselves from worldly distractions.

- In Luke 10:38-42 Jesus commends Mary for sitting at his feet while at the same time he mildly rebukes Martha for letting busyness rob her of what was most important. Mary gave Jesus her full presence. Martha gave Jesus her partial presence. She was there in body, but her soul was preoccupied with cooking dinner and her anger at Mary for not helping. Mary was mindful of Jesus. Martha was not. Her mind flitted from cooking to Mary to Jesus to her anger and then again to cooking to Mary to Jesus to her anger.

- In Psalm 131:2 the psalmist describes stilling and quieting his soul like a weaned child with his mother. As a weaned child finds contentment from simply being with his mother, so does a believer find contentment when he's mindful about the Lord.

- Isaiah 26:3 says that if we steadfastly keep our minds on the Lord, he will give us his peace. The word *steadfast* means to lean upon. Mindfulness helps us lean into and upon the Lord more consistently.

- In Matthew 6:25-30 Jesus commands us not to worry about tomorrow. Jesus preached this passage outside as part of what we call the Sermon on the Mount. As he taught about worry, he may have pointed to the birds that flew by and to flowers in the ground nearby as object lessons, drawing the attention of those listening to the here and now, the present moment, to teach these important spiritual truths.

- In 1 Kings 19 God told Elijah to stand on the mountain, for God was about to appear. God spoke not in the whirlwind or the earthquake or the fire. Rather, he spoke in a gentle whisper. It required that Elijah pay careful attention in the moment to hear God in that whisper.

Leaders should practice mindfulness as a way of life, not limit it to a devotional exercise. However, I've found that including a simple mindfulness exercise in my morning devotions helps me stay more mindful during the day. It's based on the acronym BEETS (Body Awareness, Environment Awareness, Emotions Awareness, Thought Awareness, Soul Awareness). Here's how I use it. As I begin my morning devotions, I quiet myself then mentally go through each letter and concept. It takes ten to fifteen minutes, and it's well worth it.

In one research project of eighty-seven pastor-leaders I did in 2013, those leaders who did the BEETS exercise at least once a day for five days saw a decrease in their self-reported emotional reactivity. Although they only did it for one week, they experienced a tangible benefit. This mindfulness practice can clearly help leaders stay in and experience the present moment. Here are four key concepts to keep in mind about mindfulness.

- **Intention:** While not a technique to distract ourselves, mindfulness helps us intentionally pay attention to the present moment.

- **Presence:** It is attending to what *is* at the moment rather than attending to what we want different *in* that moment. It is choosing to not ruminate over disappointment, past hurts, broken dreams, or the uncertainties of the future.

- **Nonjudgmental:** It is openness and receptivity to the moment while refusing to judge our present thoughts and emotions. Mindfulness *notices* instead of *ascribes* value to a thought or emotion. It suspends quick judgment and allows time for us to reflect.

- **Beginner's mind:** It approaches our thoughts and emotions with curiosity, like how a child might approach something new. It's a way we learn from the present and minimize the influence from preconceived biases and notions.

The Mindfulness BEETS Plan

B (Body Awareness): Check in to your body. As you pay attention to your body at this very moment, what is it telling you? Get comfortable in a chair or couch and be sure to get in a place where you won't be interrupted. Close your eyes and ask the Lord to help you focus your attention. Starting at your feet, mentally envision a scanner slowly moving up through your body: your feet, your legs, your torso, your fingers, your arms, your shoulders, your neck, and your head. Try to become aware of any body sensations such as tenseness, tightness, soreness, a clenched jaw, an aching joint, a tight muscle, and so on. As you detect any of these, try to relax yourself and get into the most comfortable position.

Reflect a few moments on this verse and tell the Lord that you want to submit your body to him today as part of God's temple.

Quote or read these verses:

Or don't you know that your body is a temple of the Holy Spirit who is in you? Don't you know that you have the Holy Spirit from God, and you don't belong to yourselves? You have been bought and paid for, so honor God with your body. (1 Cor 6:19-20)

Take about two minutes on this exercise.

E (Environment Awareness): Check in to your current surroundings. As you pay attention to your immediate environment at this very moment, what are your five senses telling you?

Next, with your eyes still closed, listen to the sounds around you. Don't just listen to the ones that immediately come to your awareness, but listen more deeply. Do you hear a clock on the wall? If you are outside, do you hear birds chirping or the rustling of leaves? Do you hear people talking? Pay attention to what your other senses are telling you. Do you feel wind on your skin? What do you smell? If you open your eyes, what are they drawn to? Focus on what your senses are telling you at this moment. Now, reflect a few moments on the following verses and thank the Lord for his creation and the five senses he's given to your body. Tell the Lord that you want to live in your world today in a God-honoring way.

Quote or read these verses.

I give thanks to you that I was marvelously set apart. Your works are wonderful—I know that very well. (Ps 139:14)

The earth's depths are in his hands; the mountain heights belong to him; the sea, which he made, is his along with the dry ground, which his own hands formed. (Ps 95:4-5)

Take one to two minutes on this exercise.

E (Emotions Awareness): Check in with your emotions. As you pay attention to your emotions at this very moment, what are they telling you? Next, pause and become aware of the emotions you are currently feeling. Are you angry, anxious, fearful, joyful, pensive, reflective, sad, happy, depressed? Whatever negative emotions you feel, acknowledge them; don't stuff them. And don't ruminate on them. Simply name them what they are. You are not judging them, just acknowledging them. Seek only to describe your emotions rather than ascribing or attaching some meaning to them. Reflect a few moments on these verses and tell God that you want to submit your emotional responses to the Spirit's control today.

Quote or read these verses:

But the fruit of the Spirit is love, joy, peace, patience, kindness, goodness, faithfulness, gentleness, and self-control. There is no law against things like this. (Gal 5:22-23)

Take about two minutes on this exercise.

116

T (Thought Awareness): Check in on your thinking. As you pay attention to your thoughts at this very moment, what are you thinking about? What are your thoughts right now? Are they about something that happened yesterday, last night, or last week? Are they about what you are planning to do today, tonight, or tomorrow? Are they about some issue in your church, family, or personal life? Are your thoughts negative or positive? As you did with your emotions, simply acknowledge your thoughts; don't judge them. Describe them rather than ascribing or attaching some meaning to them. Try to become aware of your current, real-time thoughts as an objective observer.

Reflect over this verse a few moments and tell the Lord that you want to submit your thought life to God today:

> Our weapons that we fight with aren't human, but instead they are powered by God for the destruction of fortresses. They destroy arguments, and every defense that is raised up to oppose the knowledge of God. They capture every thought to make it obedient to Christ. (2 Cor 10:4-5)

S (Soul Awareness): Check in on your soul. As you pay attention to your soul at this very moment, what is God impressing upon you? What are you sensing from him? How is he leading you?

Read these verses and ask the Lord to search your heart and prepare you to respond to God's promptings:

> The Spirit searches everything, including the depths of God. (1 Cor 2:10)

> Examine me, God! Look at my heart! Put me to the test! Know my anxious thoughts! Look to see if there is any idolatrous way in me, then lead me on the eternal path! (Ps 139:23-24)

At this point I actually begin the other parts of my devotional time, like intercessory prayer, Bible reading, and journaling.

The science behind... *Brain Surprise 7: If you're feeling down, go pet a dog. Your brain just might make you feel better.*

Multiple studies show that owning a pet increases the key neurotransmitters that make us feel better—serotonin, oxytocin, and dopamine—and even decreases the stress hormone, cortisol (Thompson, 2009). Owning a pet also decreases stress and lowers heart rate and blood pressure. In one study, owning a dog improved survival rates for heart attack victims from one in eighty-seven to one in fifteen. So if you need a boost to your motivation or mood, go buy a dog. If you buy a puppy, however, expect an uneven benefit until he quits giving you gifts on the carpet and stops howling at night.

Chapter 8

Brain-Friendly Tools That Build High-Performing Teams

Brain Surprise 8: *Being treated unfairly at work might make you sick.*

S everal years ago I lived in California's central valley where hundreds of vineyards dot the landscape. At that time my son was in high school and worked in a gun shop. He loved to duck hunt. To practice his hunting skills, he bought a homemade skeet thrower. Although I don't hunt, Josh asked me one Sunday afternoon if I wanted to join him and some of his friends to shoot skeet out in the middle of a vineyard owned by the dad of one of his friends. I jumped at the chance to spend time with him, so we hopped into our Chevy truck and headed to the vineyard.

He and his buddies set up the skeet thrower, and Josh shot a few clay pigeons to show me how it worked. He handed me the shotgun and said, "Dad, just slightly lead the disk and you'll hit it." He failed to tell me that I was supposed to snugly push the butt of the shotgun against my shoulder. Having never fired a shotgun before, I held it loosely on my shoulder and yelled, "Pull!" Two seconds later I pulled the trigger and felt a searing pain shoot through my shoulder. I had just discovered that a shotgun has a hefty kickback. I shot one more round. As my shoulder throbbed with pain, I decided skeet shooting was not for me.

While his friends continued to blast clay disks into smithereens, I strolled through the vineyard, whose vines were bursting with grapes soon to be harvested. I plucked one from a vine and tasted it. I don't think I've ever tasted a sweeter grape.

As I continued to walk, I noticed how the grapes were organized around the vines. I'd seen grapes in the grocery store, but had never been close up to them while they still hung on the vine. It struck me that although each grape was a separate entity, no grape ever hung alone. If it did, it was stunted. Every grape was always nestled in a cluster along with other grapes. And although it had its own identity, it always shared a common branch with the other grapes in that cluster. Similarly, each cluster didn't hang all by itself either. Each one shared the vine's main trunk with the other clusters.

As I reflected on my skeet-shooting/vineyard experience, I realized a parallel between good leaders and grapevines. Good leaders recognize that although those in their organization are individuals, they are also part of a team, a cluster of other individuals. The very nature of *team-ness* implies that they share a common branch, or tasks to which their team is assigned. And each team shares a common trunk with other teams as well, the organization's values, goals, objectives, and mission. The scriptures also use a vine metaphor in John 15 to describe how believers produce fruit by staying connected to the vine, or trunk, which symbolizes Jesus.

That experience that day gave me this next metaphor that illustrates brain-friendly concepts necessary for high-performing teams, **GRAPES**. In this chapter I use this acronym to describe six shared social practices that wise leaders will model and infuse into their teams to build them into high-performing ones. **GRAPES** represents these practices.

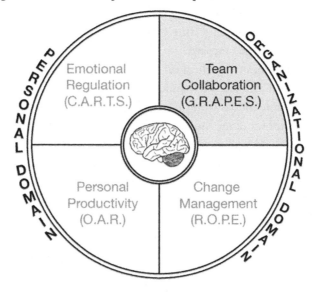

🍇 Golden rule (your team)

🍇 Reduce ambiguity (in your culture)

🍇 Allow freedom (in the workplace)

🍇 Promote personal value (among staff/volunteers)

🍇 Encourage community

🍇 Smile a lot

Strong, healthy, and cohesive teams provide the backbone for a growing business, ministry, or church. Neuroscience is providing keen insights about how we can most effectively develop our teams. From 2006 to 2008 Dr. David Rock interviewed many leading neuroscientists and summarized hundreds of neuroscience papers into a model for team collaboration that he calls SCARF. SCARF stands for five primary areas of human social experience that activate either "reward" or "threat" responses in our brains and influence our behavior (Rock, 2008). SCARF stands for status, certainty, autonomy, relatedness, and fairness. He defines those domains in these ways:

- "**S**tatus is about relative importance to others."

- "**C**ertainty concerns being able to predict the future [to some degree]."

- "**A**utonomy provides a sense of control over" one's environment and events.

- "**R**elatedness is a sense of safety with others, of friend rather than foe."

- "**F**airness is a perception of fair exchanges between people" (Rock, 2008, p. 1, emphasis added).

These qualities complement a team member or volunteer's skill competencies, gifts, experience, and educational fit for a particular role. They relate to relationships and the social culture in an organization. A model like SCARF can help leaders create a more predominant toward/reward culture and minimize away/threat influences. You'll recall the X-system (impulsive, spontaneous, emotion based) and the C-system (intentional, controlled, thinking based). Attending to the social needs of staff and volunteers helps them relate and work more consistently from their thoughtful C-systems rather than from their impulsive, emotional X-systems.

Leaders who take social needs seriously can minimize the hurtful effects that social pain causes in the workplace or among volunteers. Neuroscientists have discovered that social pain registers in the same parts of the brain that register physical pain. These parts include our *CEO*, our *Accountant*, and our *Error Detector*. They've also discovered that we can easily reexperience social pain yet not reexperience physical pain (Chen et al., 2008). In other words, we can remember facts from the past when we've been physically hurt. But when we've been socially hurt (i.e. rejected), we don't simply remember the facts, but we actually can actually reexperience the painful emotions as well.

For example, I can still remember the *pop* I heard when I blew out my knee in college while playing touch football. When I recall that experience I don't reexperience the physical pain. I simply remember catching the ball, planting my left foot to cut, and crumpling to the ground as my knee gave way. I don't feel any pain when I think about it. Yet I can still somewhat feel the emotions I felt after the game when nobody on the team offered to drive me back to my dorm. I had to hobble home by myself. Of course as time has passed, the emotions have faded. But I can quite vividly feel the emotions from more recent experiences of rejection.

Dr. Rock's model captures five significant domains that impact team collaboration and effectiveness that I believe also jibe with a biblical view of leadership. However, after I learned about this model, I wondered how well an audience of Christian leaders would embrace the SCARF model. If I taught the model to such an audience and inadvertently created a threat for Christian leaders (an "away" response), I would do the opposite of what the SCARF model intended, foster collaborative teams. If a Christian leader felt that SCARF challenged his biblical views about leadership, he could feel threatened, dismiss the model, and not experience its benefits.

For example, the word *status* presented with no context could convey to some a prideful status seeker, a self-centered person who lives as if life were all about him. In contrast to this type of status, the Bible teaches humility, putting others first: "Don't do anything for selfish purposes, but with humility think of others as better than yourselves" (Phil 2:3). The word *autonomy* could possibly imply an independent spirit and unbiblical self-reliance. However, the scriptures teach dependence on God: "Trust in the LORD with all your heart; don't rely on your own intelligence" (Prov 3:5); and interdependence: for "you are the body of Christ and parts of each other" (1 Cor 12:27).

I realized that to make my audience most receptive to these neuroscience concepts, I would need to present them in such a way as to encourage a "toward/reward" response. You'll recall that much of our social behavior is largely and unconsciously driven by our desire to minimize threat and maximize reward (Gordon, 2000). I would also need to help Christian leaders connect these concepts to their existing theology of leadership since we learn best when we can connect new knowledge to existing knowledge.

To test my hunch, I completed a small research project. Sixty-one pastor-leaders participated. They filled out an online survey using the definitions of the SCARF domains mentioned earlier. In a pre-survey they were asked to indicate to what degree they believed each of the five statements that summarized each domain was compatible with scripture. I then rewrote these concepts around a biblical framework and sent it to the pastors along with the survey. I asked them to read the rewritten concepts and then to retake the survey. Here are the results.

In the pre-survey the pastors agreed that "certainty" and "fairness" aligned with a scriptural perspective of leadership. They were neutral about "autonomy." And they disagreed that "status" and "relatedness" reflected a scriptural perspective. However, in the post-survey both "status" and "relatedness" significantly increased because I tied the terms to a biblical framework. When I presented these neuroscience concepts in a biblical context, the pastors were able to see their compatibility with a biblical leadership view.

In this chapter I suggest six neuroscience, biblically based insights described with the acronym *GRAPES* that can help leaders develop strong, healthy, collaborative teams.

Golden Rule Your Team

One of the most quoted scriptures, the Golden Rule, summarizes how we all yearn to be treated fairly. Jesus spoke these words in his famous sermon called the Sermon on the Mount: "Therefore, you should treat people in the same way that you want people to treat you" (Matt 7:12). As we all understand, this scripture implies that the way we want to be treated should guide how we treat others. And great leaders will model and build the Golden Rule into their leadership culture to foster fairness.

To show how our brains respond when we're treated fairly or unfairly, neuroscientists use a game called the Ultimatum Game (Tabibnia et al., 2008). Essentially it entails one participant making a monetary offer to a second participant. The one who makes the offer determines how much to offer and how much to keep for himself. The recipient then determines the offer's fairness and whether or not to accept it. During this game scientists look at fMRI brain scans to see what parts of the brain light up with perceived fair and unfair offers.

These studies show that when we believe we (or others) are treated fairly, we experience a strong *toward* response that can build team cohesiveness. The researchers also discovered that when we feel we've been treated unfairly, the insula lights up as well as our brain's *Error Detector* (anterior cingulate cortex). Our insula receives information from the body linked to the sensation of disgust. So, unfairness feels disgusting and can literally leave a bitter taste in our mouths. They also discovered that when someone who treated another unfairly is punished, the *Rewarder-Motivator* (ventral striatum) lights up.

Apparently God has deeply embedded into our brains our desire to be treated fairly, to experience the Golden Rule from others. When participants played the Ultimatum Game and received what they deemed as fair offers, the part of their brain associated with fundamental rewards such as food lit up (Tabibnia et al., 2008). So fairness and unfairness can powerfully influence relationships in the workplace, thus enhancing team productivity.

In addition to the Golden Rule, other scriptures also reinforce fairness. Proverbs 1:3 reminds us that Proverbs was written so that we might do what is "righteous, just, and full of integrity." In a church where I served as senior pastor, one staff member felt that I was applying a double standard about work hours. He felt that I unfairly allowed him to work fewer hours than everyone else. He perceived this as unfair, which negatively affected his view of me and caused conflict between the employee that appeared to work less and the other employees. Our team could never be cohesive unless this was addressed. At the time, unbeknownst to the concerned employee, I had placed clear expectations on the other employee about his work hours. In retrospect, knowing what I now know about fairness, I probably should have been more forthcoming to the concerned employee about what I had done. By doing so, he could have seen that I was practicing the Golden Rule and not creating an unfair situation (i.e., allowing a double standard for hours worked). Unfortunately, even perceived unfairness can hurt a team's effectiveness.

Brain-Friendly Application Tips

- *Authentically model and communicate fairness to your team.* They need to know you treat everyone fairly. If you don't, it could even affect their health. One meta-analysis (a study of studies) discovered that unfairness can actually negatively impact your team members' physical and mental health (Robbins et al., 2012).

- *Find ways to build trust.* The more trust you build with your team, the easier they'll be able to deal with any feelings of unfairness you may unintentionally create by your decisions (Delgado et al., 2005). As a result they will give you more grace.

- *When an employee or a volunteer goes beyond the call of duty, appropriately recognize his or her work.* If you don't, you may unintentionally engender an *away* response because that person may feel that you unfairly ignored his or her extra work.

- Periodically offer anonymous surveys to your team to gauge how they perceive your fairness. Depending on what you find, make appropriate adjustments.

Reduce Ambiguity in Your Culture

The brain loves certainty and predictability. It actually acts like a prediction machine (Schultz et al., 1997). It wants to know what's next. And it will fill in knowledge blanks by approximating to give it a sense of certainty. Certainty and information feels rewarding because certainty gives the brain a nice boost of dopamine, the reward neurotransmitter. To see how the brain predicts, read the following paragraph out loud.

I cnduo't bvleiee taht I culod aulaclty uesdtannrd waht I was rdnaieg. Unisg the icndeblire pweor of the hmuan mnid, aocdcrnig to rseecrah at Cmabrigde Uinervtisy, it dseno't mttaer in waht oderr the lteters in a wrod are, the olny irpoamtnt tihng is taht the frsit and lsat ltteer be in the rhgit pclae. The rset can be a taotl mses and you can sitll raed it whoutit a pboerlm. Tihs is bucseae the huamn mnid deos not raed ervey ltteer by istlef, but the wrod as a wlohe. Aaznmig, huh?

What did you notice? Surprisingly, you probably noticed that you could read it. And you may also have realized that the letters of each word were jumbled except for the first and last letter. Your brain filled in the blanks because it seeks certainty and recognizes patterns. It created certainty by filling in the words so you could read the paragraph.

However, when the brain deals with the opposite of certainty, which is ambiguity, it can feel like a threat. And threats create away responses. Our brain's *Error Detector* engages, which can lead to our *Panic Alarm* running things rather than our *CEO* (Rosen & Donley, 2006). Uncertainty affects our brains in several ways:

- We assume the worst and fill in the knowledge gaps with negative information (Hsu et al., 2005).
- We delay decisions (Pilay, 2011, Kindle e-book loc. 4110).
- The reward neurotransmitter, dopamine, decreases (Platt & Huettel, 2008).
- We get distracted from the task at hand because the *Accountant* engages and siphons away energy resources from our *CEO* (Hedden & Gabrieli, 2006).
- Team productivity decreases (Herry et al., 2007).
- Our memory gets clouded because uncertainty creates stress that can affect memory.

If your team lives in constant uncertainty, it can cause chronic stress and diminish team performance. In chapter 6, I explained that *allostatic load* refers to the wear and tear on the body from chronic stress. Chronic stress not only affects memory but also destroys neurons, stifles new neuron growth (neurogenesis), and inhibits the body's ability to regulate the stress hormone cortisol. If incessant unpredictability describes your workplace environment, your team will be more sensitive to threat, which will in turn affect their performance. This diagram shows how our bodies and ultimately our team's performance respond to uncertainty.

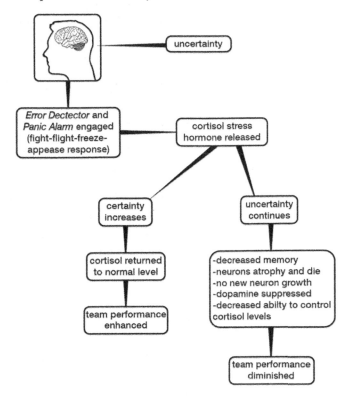

Continual uncertainty will diminish your team's performance. And although the brain does not like uncertainty, the scriptures speak to its reality. The Bible teaches that we live in a world often filled with uncertainty because ultimately we don't know what tomorrow holds. When uncertainty gets the best of us, worry results. And Jesus tells us not to worry about tomorrow (Matt 6) because our faith in him gives us certainty. "Faith is the reality of what we hope for, the proof of what we don't see" (Heb 11:1). God's promises are certain because God does not lie (Num 23:19), and his promises are a yes to you in Jesus Christ. "All of God's promises have their yes in him" (2 Cor 1:20). In addition, the Bible often uses vivid metaphors of things to illustrate God's faithfulness and dependability: He is our rock (Matt 16:18), our foundation (1 Cor 3:11), a tower to which we can run (Prov 18:10).

🧠 *Brain-Friendly Application Tips*

- *Minimize ambiguity about what you expect from your team.* Be clear about expectations and team roles. The less ambiguous your expectations of the team, the more effectively they'll perform (Cicero et al., 2010).

- *Overcommunicate.* In the absence of information, your team will fill in the gaps incorrectly. Keep people informed.

- When your organization faces ambiguities, try to *create more certainty* by turning the ambiguities into probabilities by creating timelines, milestones, and potential solutions.

- *Set regular goals.* Goals are one way we can create certainty about the future. Break down goals into smaller components so that your team can regularly see progress. Each win will create a reward response in the brain, which in turn further motivates us.

- *Recognize that some people need more certainty than others* (Ford & Collins, 2010). The more conservative your church, the less tolerant they are of ambiguity. Stay flexible in how you manage ambiguous situations from person to person. Team members who tend to be anxious (Bishop, 2007) or struggle with their self-esteem (Ford & Collins, 2010) also tend to be less tolerant of ambiguity. A single method of dealing with ambiguity with your team members won't fit all.

- As a leader, *be consistent in how you carry yourself* and how you show up at work or in ministry settings. Don't leave people wondering what mood they'll find you in each day.

🍇 Allow Freedom in the Workplace

When I use the word *freedom*, I mean that you give your team choices, unlike the zombie figures in the iconic Macintosh ad that debuted in the 1984 Super Bowl. Freedom means that you intentionally create an atmosphere that provides choices to your team. When we believe that we have choices, it's rewarding simply in itself (Rock & Cox, 2012). When employees or volunteers experience freedom and autonomy, it empowers them. However, in environments where people have little freedom, like the Apple commercial zombies, it saps motivation and energy.

Several studies have shown many positive benefits when workers experience freedom and autonomy. Postal workers given more decision-making authority in Norway scored higher on overall health (Mikkelsen & Gundersen, 2003). Nursing home residents live longer when given more choices about their living space (Thomas, 1996). Franchisee owners say that freedom to make their own choices played a major role in their decision to own their own business (Baron & Schmidt, 1991). When patients connected to a morphine drip had the option to press the morphine button versus having to call the nurse to get it, they required less morphine because their freedom of choice helped them tolerate pain better (Mackie et al., 1991). Even an illusion of autonomy decreases activation in the brain's *Panic Alarm* (Salomens et al., 2007). On the other hand, when someone is in a constant state of no freedom, helplessness, they are very likely to get hypertension (Stern et al., 2009). So, freedom and autonomy are also good for the body.

In chapter 4 we looked at the brain's basic building block, the brain cell called the neuron. At one end of each neuron lie tiny branches called dendrites that receive signals from other neurons. In some cases, the more of these branches, the better neurons can communicate, the better our brain functions, and the more productive we are. In other cases, however, when we lack freedom and autonomy in the workplace, stress results, as happens with uncertainty, seen in the previous diagram. That stress in turn atrophies the branches in our *Rememberer* (hippocampus) yet grows them in our amygdala (Magariños et al., 1996), the flight-fight part of our *Panic Alarm* (not good). So team members with little freedom are more apt to be controlled by their brain's *Panic Alarm*. You could replace uncertainty with lack of freedom in the stress diagram and still get the same results.

God's word shows us that God gave us a free will to make independent choices each day. We are not automatons. God gives us freedom to follow Jesus within the boundaries of the word. We must daily choose whom we will follow (Josh 25:15). Yet we are not to live life independently. In 1 Corinthians 12 the New Testament uses the human body as a metaphor for the church. Just as each part of the human body mutually depends upon the other parts, so are Christians mutually dependent upon each other. Although we are independent (autonomous up to a point) we are also interdependent upon each other. We need each other.

Brain-Friendly Application Tips

- *Give staff and volunteers choices in how they perform their role.* You could give them reasonable flexibility in how they set up their workplace or the steps they take to accomplish agreed-upon goals. Such flexibility can foster a sense of well-being among the team members (Leotti & Delgado, 2011).

- *Guard against micromanaging your team.* Give them direction, but don't breathe down their necks. Periodically ask them if they feel properly managed or overmanaged.

- *Monitor your team's stress level.* The more stressed they feel, the less empathy and patience they'll be able to show to fellow team members (Rameson et al., 2012) because it takes intentional effort to empathize. As a result, team productivity can be affected and relational conflict can rise.

- *Find what intrinsically motivates team members and give them assignments in those areas.* They'll be more satisfied and more productive (Lee & Reeve, 2012). People feel more motivated when they enjoy what they do.

Promote Personal Value among Staff and Volunteers

When a leader helps his team members feel more valued, he can create a *toward* state that boosts team collaboration. The SCARF model uses the word *status* instead of the word *value*, which I prefer. Status received the lowest rating from the pastors who took my survey probably because the word could imply unbiblical comparison. The Bible tells us not to compare (2 Cor 10:12). For when we compare, we could become envious of others or become prideful and take pleasure in another's misfortune, a term called *Schadenfreude*, which unfortunately gives the brain a boost of dopamine (Takahashi et al., 2009). Apparently there's a brain basis for the saying *revenge is sweet*.

In contrast to the effects of unbiblical comparison, the Bible commands us to avoid envy (Gal 5:19-21) and to *share* the pain of others when they experience misfortune (Rom 12:15), not be glad about it. In fact, envy not only is sinful but actually elicits a threat response in our brains (Rock & Cox, 2012).

130

And when we compare ourselves to others or when we don't feel valued, stress results, which in turn dampens our *CEO* and heightens our *Panic Alarm's* sensitivity (Prabhakaran & Gray, 2012). As we're now seeing, ignoring any domain in the *GRAPES* model can result in stress and diminished team performance.

On the other hand, Christianity has elevated the status of those throughout history who have been relegated to society's lower rungs.

- The shepherds: They were the first to be told of the birth of Jesus even though they were at the lowest end of the social scale (Luke 2).

- Women: They were the first to see Jesus's empty tomb, although during the biblical era their testimony was not accepted in court (Setzer, 1997, p. 259). In contrast, the Bible accepted their testimony.

- The disadvantaged: The Bible encourages us to care for widows and orphans (Jas 1:27), as well as prisoners and the homeless (Matt 25:36).

- Those in general considered low in society: the Apostle Paul highlighted that God chose and elevated those who weren't considered wise, influential, or worthy in the eyes of the world to show God's grace (1 Cor 1:26-31).

The Bible also commands us to build a good reputation with others, one measure of status. "A good reputation is better than much wealth; high esteem is better than silver and gold" (Prov 22:1). A good reputation and respect from others is also a nonnegotiable quality required from all leaders (1 Tim 3:7). A good reputation actually feels good because it activates our brain's *Rewarder-Motivator* (Izuma et al., 2008). Studies also show that respect from others improves our overall sense of well-being more than the proverbial *keeping up with the Joneses* measure of status (Anderson et al., 2012).

So how can a leader promote personal value (increase status) to help create *toward* states in his team? Consider these tips.

Brain-Friendly Application Tips

- *Regularly tell your team members that you value them.* Thank them often. Tell them how valuable their contributions are

131

even though their jobs may not be viewed as important as other ones. Use tangible expressions of appreciation. Discover what uniquely gives them a sense of value and communicate thanks in that way. The highest performing teams receive a ratio of six positive comments to one negative one (Ko, 2012). However, praise should focus on effort, such as hard work, rather than attributes, such as intelligence. Praise for effort keeps your team open to grow, whereas praise for attributes can sometimes cause the person to become static to protect his or her attributes (Rock, 2011).

- *Help them make progress in their work.* Support them so that they feel they are making headway. In one study, over six hundred managers recorded at the end of each day the experiences that satisfied them the most. Progress on their goals and tasks satisfied them most, even more than receiving praise or recognition (Amabile et al., 2010).

- *Teach your team what healthy comparison looks like*: comparing personal effort against their own efforts, rather than against the efforts of other team members. Talk about the downsides of seeking status through comparison. Help them learn to recognize when they begin to compare themselves with others.

- Develop a thorough *orientation process for new team members, paid and volunteer.* This will increase the value those new team members will feel.

- *Value the insight and input from your team.* Help your team realize that we naturally default to believing others see things as we ourselves do. It's called the false consensus effect. Foster a healthy, open atmosphere so that everybody on the team feels free to share his or her views (Ross et al., 1977). Foster an atmosphere that not only gives everybody a chance to share their opinions but welcomes their opinions as well. When you do, everybody can get a boost of another nice neurotransmitter, oxytocin, which lowers activation in the brain's *Panic Alarm* and builds collaboration (Baumgartner et al., 2008).

132

🍇 Encourage Community

God created us with a strong need for community. The concept of community fills the pages of the scriptures. The Godhead of the Trinity (Matt 28:19) represents community. The Hebrew people throughout the Old Testament represent it. The New Testament models community (Acts 2:42) and commands it (Heb 10:25).

Some even believe that our hunger for community is as strong as our need for the basics of life like food (Cacioppo & Patrick, 2009). And when we don't experience community and we feel excluded or rejected, the pain we feel actually engages the same part of our brains that registers physical pain (Eisenberger, 2012). Not only does our own social pain register in our brains, but when we see others rejected, our brain's pain centers light up as well (Beeney et al., 2011).

No one likes to feel excluded, to be seen as part of the "out" group. Jesus perfectly understood our need to belong and was often criticized for reaching out to those in society's "out" group, who were often excluded. Several times the scriptures describe the Pharisees' disdain for Jesus's inclusion of society's down-and-outers.

- He spent time with tax collectors, whom the Jews in biblical days hated. He even picked one, Matthew, to be one of his disciples (Matt 9:9-11).

- He touched lepers, considered unclean by society (Matt 8).

- He allowed a prostitute to anoint his head with perfume and wash his feet with her hair and tears (Mark 14).

- He went to parties with those considered sinners (Luke 5:29-30).

Jesus extended love and acceptance to those who desperately needed community. He welcomed all who would listen to his message, follow him, and allow him to transform their lives. In fact, he often contrasted the "out" group (the sinners), with the so-called "in" group (the Pharisees). He wanted to bring those who needed a savior into his family, into community with himself and his followers, through repentance and faith.

Leaders must be acutely aware of these dynamics in the workplace and prioritize community building. I recall one painful experience when I felt pushed

133

out of community. It definitely activated my brain's *Panic Alarm*. In one church-staff position from which I was transitioning, I stayed a few extra months to assist the church during that transition. Each Tuesday the staff would eat lunch together and then pray at the end. At the beginning of this transition, a pastor who was put in charge of those lunch prayer meetings pulled me aside and asked me to not attend them anymore. I was shocked but acquiesced. To this day I'm not sure why he asked me not to attend, but I surmise he wanted to give the staff freedom to discuss how they'd handle my move into a new ministry.

I recall several Tuesday lunchtimes as I sat in my office, eating alone at my desk while the rest of the staff ate lunch and held their prayer meeting in the conference room, a few offices away. Because the building was poorly insulated, I could often hear their laughter waft into my office. I had to fight back tears because I felt deeply excluded from the "in" group.

I'm sure that pastor didn't intentionally hurt me. Yet I felt incredible social pain during those lonely lunch hours. Social pain is so strong that we even use the same kinds of terms to describe it as we do for physical pain, terms such as a *broken heart* or *hurt feelings*. In fact, one study of fifteen different language groups found that words used to describe social pain are largely taken from those that describe physical pain (Macdonald & Leary, 2005). Social pain and the feelings of exclusion do not respect nationality, race, gender, or language. This same social pain and its effects can happen unintentionally in any workplace environment unless the leader encourages community.

When we feel that we share things in common with our team, that we are similar, that we belong, and that we like each other, productivity increases (Walton et al., 2012). Belonging even makes it easier to deal with perceived inequity that sometimes arises in a team (Parboteeah et al., 2005). While respecting and appreciating differences, shared team values and shared wins can create deeper relational connections because the values the team holds feel like each individual's own values. And when one team member wins, it feels like a win to everybody (Mobbs et al., 2009). The scriptures also speak to this shared experience in Romans 12:15, when we are told to "be happy with those who are happy." Here's how to build deeper community into your team.

Brain-Friendly Application Tips

- *Provide regular relationship-building experiences* for your teams to deepen their chemistry and their friendships. Foster the sense that nobody is in the "out" group. If some team members are perceived to be in the "out" group, it can set up a subtle prejudice that can affect team dynamics (Dhont et al., 2011). Teach your team that because we naturally default to seeing others as being in the "out" group, your team must be vigilant to avoid it. Monitor for cliques. Be vigilant especially when you bring new team members on board.

- *Create physical gathering places* in the workplace that encourage socialization. Something as simple as water cooler conversations can help build community (Robison, 2008).

- Regularly *remind your team to see other team members' perspectives.* Teach them to learn to walk in other team members' shoes. It's called mentalizing, and I mentioned it in the last chapter. Mentalizing helps us see situations from the perspective of others. Studies show that the more we do this, the more likely we are to feel empathy toward and relate more positively to those whose perspective we are taking (Waytz et al., 2012).

- *Help team members share goals.* When they share goals, their connection to each other and their commitment to the team's goals will intensify (Shteynberg & Galinsky, 2011).

- *Build an attitude of gratitude* among your team. Model gratitude so that your team can see it in you. Regularly explain how gratitude not only is biblical but also helps build team cohesiveness (Lambert et al., 2010).

- *Use appropriate humor.* People endear themselves to those with a good sense of humor (Bippus, 2000).

- Again *build trust.* As trust increases, oxytocin increases, which strengthens cooperativeness among your team (De Dreu, 2012) and empathy toward each other (Meyer-Lindenberg et al., 2011). It even lowers blood pressure and the amount of the stress hormone, cortisol, in our bodies (Glasser, 2013).

🍇 Smile a Lot

This last practice in the GRAPES model, *smile a lot,* may initially seem trite. Yet the act of smiling captures the importance of a discovery of a group of neurons called *mirror neurons*. These neurons, also called our brains' resonance circuits, give credibility to the truism that followers mirror their leaders.

In the 1960s, scientists at the University of Parma in Italy discovered these interesting brain cells almost by accident (Gallese et al., 1996). They had implanted a probe into the motor cortex of a monkey's brain to study motor movements. When the monkey reached for a peanut, specific neurons would fire. But they also discovered that those same neurons fired when the monkey simply *observed* the researchers reach for a peanut. In other words, the monkey's brain reacted in the same way as if he actually had reached for the food. Thus these neurons got the name *mirror neurons*. Although people understandably don't volunteer for such experiments on their own brains, fMRI studies show that we humans also have mirror neurons. Although many neuroscientists believe mirror neurons exist, there is still some controversy about them (Hickok, 2009).

When we see others feel an emotion or take some intentional action, in contrast to a random action, these neuron areas activate just as if it were our own experience (Rizzolatti & Sinigaglia, 2008). In other words, we mirror the purposeful actions of others. Someone smiles at us and we smile back. Likewise, when we see someone grimace, we grimace. When we see someone get an injection on a TV show, we turn our heads to avoid feeling that pain ourselves. When somebody yawns, we often yawn. Even a baby just a few hours old will mimic her mother by sticking out her tongue if her mother sticks out hers (Dobbs, 2006).

Daniel Goleman, who popularized emotional intelligence, said this about mirror neurons: "Mirror neurons have particular importance in organizations, because leaders' emotions and actions prompt followers to mirror those feelings and deeds. The effects of activating neural circuitry in followers' brains can be very powerful" (Goleman & Boyatzis, 2008). In other words, a leader's actions, demeanor, and emotions are contagious and will snowball in the workplace and in ministry settings. It's called emotional contagion.

The scriptures speak to the power of a leader's demeanor. Proverbs 16:15 describes the power ancient kings wielded: "There's life in the light of the king's face. His favor is like a cloud that brings spring rain." When an ancient king smiled at someone, it implied that his favor was on that person, which would *refresh* the subject's spirit. The opposite was also true. Leaders embody that same kind of power with their body language, tone of voice, facial expression, and actions. The tone they set will ripple through an entire team.

When we *ripple out* good moods and emotions, it improves performance and cooperation and decreases conflict (Barsade, 2002).

I experienced this ripple effect a few years ago at a new hot dog deli that opened up near my home. I had heard they made a great Chicago dog and cooked some great fries so I decided I'd try it one day for lunch. The first thing I noticed when I walked in was a scowl cemented on the cashier's face and on the rest of the employees' faces as well. He gruffly asked me what I wanted, and because I halted a bit, being unfamiliar with their menu, he acted peeved at my slowness. I finally placed the order for two hot dogs and a medium order of fries. I paid him and stepped back as he prepared the order.

When I got my bag, I noticed I didn't get the fries I had ordered. After I pointed that out, he grabbed the sack, walked back to the young cook, and yelled at him. His cook barked something back at him. Every patron in the deli felt the negative vibe that filled the deli. He finally corrected my order and almost threw the sack back at me. I then realized that the cashier was the owner himself. Every employee in the deli took on the owner's gruff demeanor. I never bought another hot dog there again.

In a similar way, your team will mimic you. The Apostle Paul often wrote about our need to provide a good model for others. He said that believers should follow his example and that they should set good examples for others as well (1 Cor 11:1; Phil 3:17; 1 Tim 4:12). A leader's intentional actions, when seen by others, can profoundly affect a team's effectiveness, both in a good and a bad way.

Mirror neurons reinforce the power of imitation. They help us perform our own virtual-reality simulations of the intentions of others and to mimic their actions. They also help create shared social experiences. Many neuroscientists believe that they help us empathize with others (Iacoboni, 2009). Empathy gives us the ability to tune in to the emotions of others, feel what others feel, and take the other person in to account, although research is still ongoing to determine how strongly mirror neurons influence empathy (Decety, 2010).

A friend once told me about one of her clients. The client had recently become the CEO of a very large firm. The prior CEO had treated his employees unfairly, and the hurt still lingered after the new boss arrived. My friend shared that the new boss spent the first few weeks grasping the severity of the situation. He then called an all-employee meeting in the company auditorium. During that meeting, in a humble and genuine way, he told them that he had discovered how poorly they had been treated by the prior CEO. But he went one step further. He didn't simply state the facts. He showed how he felt; tears ran down his cheeks; he had felt their anger and pain. My friend then shared that at that exact moment the new CEO reported that he could feel those employees palpably connect to him. He didn't force empathy. It flowed genuinely from his heart.

Wise leaders, armed with an understanding of mirror neurons, can powerfully influence their team through empathy, their demeanor, and their actions in these ways.

Brain-Friendly Application Tips

- When dealing with staff persons or volunteers who are in emotional pain, *ask the Lord to help you genuinely empathize* with them. Mirror their pain through your facial expressions, but not artificially. If you fake it, their mirror neurons may pick up on your insincerity. I once was in a meeting with a leader who had treated me very poorly. He began to cry after I shared I was willing to yield on a position. I felt his tears were forced and that he was disingenuous. However, when you genuinely connect through facial expressions and emotion, you can create a deeper connection with your team.

- *Pay attention to the facial expressions and body language of others.* Guard against ramrodding ideas without considering team members' demeanor. Look for subtle clues that may indicate you need to discuss the issue further before proceeding. Seek to be fully present with them.

- *Stay aware of your own demeanor.* One study on facial expressions discovered that a disapproving look activates the flight-fight part of our brain, the amygdala, even more than an angry look (Burklund et al., 2007).

- When communicating key initiatives or changes, *maximize face-to-face communication.* If you only rely on e-mail, print, or online communication, you lose the ability to read your team's facial expressions and important cues. In addition, your team will more clearly understand your intentions when they see your facial expressions. Remember, mirror neurons help us sense the intentions of others, and being physically present helps us understand others better.

- When in a meeting with someone whose anger is rising to an unhealthy level, *guard against mirroring back a similar angry scowl.* Mirror back calmness. Intervene if necessary by calling for a break in the meeting. Sometimes a leader must stop the mirroring of destructive or anxious emotions and actions.

- *Chill out.* Learn to relax around your team. Use humor, and as the "S" in the acronym says, smile a lot. Studies show that teams rate more highly those leaders who use humor well (Sala, 2003). Just as humor builds community, it also reinforces the power of mirror neurons. And laughter can even help your team process information more effectively.

One final note about this chapter's content: regularly teach your team about these six social needs. Often staff and volunteers can unintentionally do things that create threat responses from others. So the more you can remind your team about these concepts, the more likely they'll implement them. The more you can create a *toward/reward* leadership culture, the more your team members will want to work with each other and collaborate. And, if one area of the *GRAPES* model suffers from time to time, often you can compensate by strengthening another area. In the example I shared about one employee feeling that I was unfair about work hours, I could have compensated by providing some social experiences the entire team could have shared together.

I close this chapter with a brief excerpt from *My Utmost for His Highest* by Oswald Chambers. He picks up on the ultimate mirroring a Christian leader should seek, mirroring the life of Christ.

All of us are looking with unveiled faces at the glory of the Lord as if we were looking in a mirror. We are being transformed into that same image from one degree of glory to the next degree of glory. This comes from the Lord, who is the Spirit. (2 Cor 3:18)

The greatest characteristic a Christian can exhibit is this completely un-veiled openness before God, which allows that person's life to become a mirror for others. When the Spirit fills us, we are transformed, and by be-holding God we become mirrors. You can always tell when someone has been beholding the glory of the Lord, because your inner spirit senses that he mirrors the Lord's own character. Beware of anything that would spot or tarnish that mirror in you. It is almost always something good that will stain it—something good, but not what is best. (Chambers, 1992, p. 22)

The science behind...*Brain Surprise 8*: *Being treated unfairly at work might make you sick. (De Boer et al., 2002)*

In one study of 514 security guards, researchers discovered that if em-ployees felt they weren't being treated fairly at work, their absenteeism rate would increase. Health issues were behind much of this absenteeism. So if you have someone who is missing a lot of days due to less-than-acute health reasons, perhaps you need to discover if that employee feels that he or she is being treated unfairly.

Chapter 9

Sticky Change and the Brain

Brain Surprise 9: *If you're feeling rejected, your brain can make you feel better if you take two Tylenol tablets.*

I had arrived and I was going to change our community by planting the megachurch of the South, or so I thought.

Several years earlier I had attended seminary while working as a singles' minister at a large and thriving church in Fort Worth, Texas. After graduation I left to serve as an associate pastor at an even larger church in Oklahoma. My wife and I relished this new opportunity. My vocational career path was looking up.

While there I began my doctor of ministry at Trinity Evangelical Divinity Seminary in Deerfield, Illinois, and met a student who planned to plant a church in Florida. God used that relationship to stir in me a desire to start a church in what at that time was the fastest-growing county in the United States, Gwinnett County just outside Atlanta. Three years later we resigned from our church in Oklahoma to begin the new one. My initial financial commitment from supporters totaled one hundred dollars a month plus a borrowed gas credit card I could use for six months. Yet I had faith that God was going to do great things.

I had heard about Rick Warren's story of Saddleback Church in California, which grew into a megachurch of several thousand. I believed I would experience similar success. I envisioned an amazing story that out of my home Bible study of a few adults would emerge this huge church. I assumed that

141

one day I'd headline church growth conferences as I shared my ministry secrets with other pastors.

When we arrived in Atlanta, I rented a dance studio for our Sunday services. I visited hundreds of homes and invited people to come to the first service. I sent out a cool flier and waited with excitement for that great day (actually it felt more like a knot in my stomach than excitement): our first public life-changing, community-transforming worship service.

I expected parking problems and overflow crowds our first Sunday. Thirty minutes prior to the start of the service, I began to pray in a small piano room tucked away to the side of the studio entrance. It was close enough for me to hear the door squeak every time someone walked in. My prayer soon became desperate as we approached the service start time. I had only counted about twenty squeaks.

We ended up with fifty-one people that day, including about fifteen in the nursery. I told myself it was a great start and that attendance would do nothing but rise from that point forward. I expected that we'd run several hundred within the year. Six months later my church plant was so successful that I had worked that initial fifty-one down to seventeen, including five in the nursery.

I'll never forget that July 4 weekend. I was devastated by the sparse attendance. As I led the music and spoke to a dozen faithful, I fought back tears. After the service ended and we cleared out the studio, I drove home in silence with my wife and kids. When we got to our drafty rental home, I trudged upstairs to our half bath. I dropped the toilet seat top down, buried my face in a bath towel, and wept. My vision to build a great church, to change the community, to reach thousands of people lay in shambles. I was a broken man. My identity was crushed. I felt like a failure. Fortunately, God gave us the grace to persevere, and over the next fourteen years God grew the church to around five hundred. But I was ignorant about change. I had no clue about how to bring about change in a person, much less in a church or in a community. I wish I'd known then what I know now about how the brain responds to change.

In this chapter I will focus on what I had missed and what many leaders miss when they try to bring change. With neuroscience as the foundation, this chapter will unpack how to make change stick and how to minimize disruption that change often causes.

Every organization must change to grow. Change means you're alive. It means your organization is healthy. Without lasting change (the kind that sticks), organizations die, sometimes quickly, sometimes slowly. Changes that leaders often face include these and more:

- Getting staff to embrace new reporting and feedback systems.

- Helping employees accept annual goals your leadership sets.

- Embracing the changes caused by globalization and technology advancement.

- Faith-based organizations responding to the dramatic change in society's moral stances on long-held biblical beliefs.

- Guiding your board to think outside the box to move your organization forward.

- Merging, cutting, or beginning new departments.

- Responding to the dynamic created when you add new staff or volunteer leaders or when key players leave your organization.

- Starting new initiatives.

- Helping staff live healthier lifestyles to reduce sick days and improve productivity.

Unfortunately, the majority of organizational change fails, performs subpar, or makes things worse (Cope, 2003). I once naively thought that I could create change simply from my position as a leader. If I announced a change, I mistakenly assumed people would magically fall into place and follow my leadership if given sufficient facts. I was surprised when they didn't. I had used the traditional carrot-and-stick "telling" approach and ignored the brain dynamics everybody experiences when they face change. In fact, many leaders today rely on the same unsuccessful methodology that Alan Deutschman describes in his book *Change or Die: The Three Keys to Change in Work and in Life*: facts, fear, and force. Brain insight, however, can help us replace unworkable change strategies and with new ones so our change initiatives become stickier and endure.

The group in which you hope to bring about change will vary depending upon your situation. You may need any of these groups to embrace change for it to be successful: administrative staff, management staff, boards, pastoral staff, and so on. To keep things simple, I will use the word *team* in the rest of this chapter to avoid restating each group's name when I talk about the group in which you hope to bring about change.

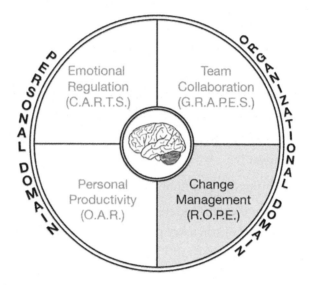

In this chapter, the model for change is called *ROPE*. You can't force anyone to move from point A to point B with a rope. But if you can persuade him or her to hold the rope and hang on, you can gently pull him to point B. That's how the *ROPE* model works to effect change. When we incorporate insight about the brain, we can help our teams choose to embrace the change rather than feel coerced.

Even Jesus didn't force others to change. He invited people to willingly choose to follow him and allow his Spirit to change them. He engaged their hearts and minds first. Behavior then followed. Likewise, *sticky* change happens when we first change our team's minds and hearts by helping them see and embrace new perspectives. Brain insight helps us do that.

The acronym *ROPE* stands for these concepts.

Recognize why the brain resists change.

 Organize your thoughts around a brain-friendly plan that others will buy into.

 Persuade with brain-friendly messaging.

 Evaluate progress through brain-friendly feedback.

Recognize Why the Brain Resists Change

Wise leaders understand that lasting change requires individuals to change first before an organization will change. Your change won't last or will disrupt your organization unless those in your teams personally embrace the change first, at least at some level. So it behooves us to first understand why most people initially resist change. Neuroscience helps us understand hidden processes around which we can design our change initiatives.

In the last chapter we looked at several brain-friendly insights that build unified and healthy teams. We learned that people want certainty and freedom because the brain craves both. Change inevitably causes uncertainty (the future will be different from what I'm used to) and fear of lost freedom. To many people change may mean, "I will have less autonomy and choice."

Here I've summarized brain processes that come into play when we try to bring change.

- People naturally assume the worst. Our brain is wired to pick up threats and negative possibilities around us more than the positive. Two-thirds of the brain cells in the flight-fight part of our brain, the amygdala, are wired to pick up on the negative (Hanson, 2010). Most people's initial response to change comes from their X-system, rather than from their C-system.

- People naturally fill in knowledge gaps with fear. Uncertainty about the future (and change) breeds this fear. The less information and the more people have to fill in the knowledge gaps, the greater the fear and resistance to change.

- Undoing a wrong impression is harder than creating a good one.

It's the adage "you don't have a second chance to make a good first impression." That's not just a quaint saying. Neuroscientists have shown it to be true (Lount et al., 2008). Poorly introduced change starts you out on the wrong footing.

- People understate their ability to ride out difficult future events (Wilson & Gilbert, 2005).

- Uncertainty causes us to poorly forecast how well we can face difficulty that changes may bring. The term is called "affective forecasting." When you present change, your team will often initially assume that things will be worse than expected, although the opposite is often true.

- Emotions play a significant role in decision making and influence how well your team will embrace change. Just presenting facts without engaging positive and hopeful emotions will seldom move your team forward.

- The brain can only handle so much change at once. Trying to create too much change too quickly can engage the brain's fear center and cause an away response, thus hindering change (Hemp, 2009).

The Tug-of-War

Personal change is hard for most of us. Our brain's built-in tendencies work against it as the previous list described. Our unconscious habits lie deep in our *Automatic Transmission* (basal ganglia). Over time repeated habits create strong neuronal connections something akin to being hardwired. Much of what we do every day operates with little conscious effort on our part. As I stated before, some estimate that over 40 percent of what we do each day is a habit, not a conscious decision (Duhigg, 2012b). It's as if our brain is on autopilot. The X-system, which doesn't tire easily nor easily get distracted, drives those automatic habits and routines. And it doesn't change very easily either, although neuroplasticity tells us that we can rewire our brain. The old saying "old habits die hard" is rooted in how the brain works.

Change, however, requires that we engage our C-system, driven primarily by our brains' *CEO* (prefrontal cortex). In contrast to the X-system, it requires more energy and tires easily. So the changes that you propose mean that your team will have to think. And since thinking is hard work and the brain prefers to take the easy route that relies on our habit centers, it's not surprising that change is hard.

It's like a tug-of-war between the familiar and easy (what we are used to, our habits) and the unfamiliar and difficult (the change). Also, since our habits are so deeply ingrained, it's often hard to put them into words since we've not had to do so for a while. For example, try to explain to someone how to ride a bike. It's difficult to find the words to do so. So when your team resists change, it may even be difficult for them to put their resistance into words. They may resist your proposed change and not really know why. It just feels wrong to them. Remember, our X-system, the feelings-oriented process, acts without thinking. So when you present change to others, their brains subconsciously engage it first, before they engage their C-system.

This tug-of-war becomes more acute as we age. Studies (and common sense) show that change becomes more difficult the older we get (Goh & Park, 2009). Our brains become less resilient, we lose some cognitive functioning, and we process information slower because, among other things, the insulation (myelin) around our neurons' pathways (axons) decreases and our dendrites also decrease. Our brains simply slow down. And they produce less dopamine, the neurotransmitter that helps us stay alert and motivated.

This growing resistance to change as we age is akin to the deep gorge cut by a river that has been flowing for centuries. To divert the flow would take tremendous energy. However, with patience and time on your part and willingness on theirs, older people can embrace change. And if they are motivated, have assumed a posture of *never quit learning*, and have sufficient social support systems, I've seen some older adults actually embrace change more quickly than younger adults.

Cognitive Dissonance

When we first hear about a proposed change that would affect us, we often experience something called "cognitive dissonance." It's the inner tension we feel when we face behaving in ways that conflict with our beliefs and habits. It makes us resistant to change, at least initially.

For example, let's say you want to change your office from a five-day-a-week schedule to a four-day-a-week schedule. You team will experience cognitive dissonance as they begin to think about their own work hours changing from 8 a.m. to 5 p.m. to 7 a.m. to 6 p.m. Several systems in their brains get activated.

The brain's *Error Detector* (anterior cingulate cortex) may engage, as well as the brain's *Panic Alarm* (limbic system). For instance, this might happen when an administrative staffer whose name we'll say is Sara thinks about the changes she'll have to make to find extended child care for her kids. On the other hand, if she thinks about the benefits of the change (an extra day off per week with her family), her *Rewarder-Motivator* (nucleus accumbens) could activate. As her brain's *Accountant* (orbitofrontal cortex) receives these conflicting signals, it would then send this information to her *CEO* (prefrontal cortex). These processes take a lot of energy and can stifle her *CEO's* ability to think clearly. The emotional side of the expected change can blur her thoughtful reflection and the benefits from those changes.

When faced with change, we will almost always initially experience cognitive dissonance. It stirs up emotional anxiety that can dampen clear thinking. Yet, seldom will the brain bypass this initial response. So as you propose changes, realize that most in your team will experience this tension.

Changing Resistance over Time

Your team's response to change can also change over time. Let's say you introduce a change that will take place a year from now in your church. You plan to add an early service on Sundays. Initially your staff sees many benefits that an early service can provide, such as more space and more service options. The negatives, such as more work, recruiting more volunteers, and a longer day, don't seem that large. Neuroscientists have discovered that when the change is far away, the positives usually outweigh the negatives (Löw et al., 2008).

However, the closer we get to the change, the more fearful we get as we think about the implications and the personal cost (i.e., "Now, I've got to get to church two hours earlier each Sunday). The cost becomes more concrete, whereas further away from the change the positives stood out more. So the closer you get to beginning the new service, the more it can feel like a threat to your staff. Uninformed optimism gives way to informed pessimism. So leaders will do well to incorporate this insight into their buy-in change plans.

Social Threats

In the last chapter on team collaboration, the GRAPES metaphor described how healthy leaders, teams, and organizations should apply these six practices. However, change actually works against the first five in these ways.

- *Golden Rule it*: change can create fear, a threat response, with concerns that when the change occurs, some may not be treated fairly.

- *Remove ambiguity*: innate to change is the unknown about the future, which creates threat.

- *Allow freedom*: change can cause an away response by the possibility that it may lessen the freedom experienced in a current role or ministry.

- *Promote individual value*: change can evoke concern about whether or not someone may be valued less in the role or ministry.

- *Encourage community*: change may create worry that relationships will become strained and community disrupted or lessened.

So as you consider your change, begin by understanding why change is so hard for the brain. For some personalities change does come more easily. Even so, many people in your team may respond to your change in the aforementioned ways. Recognizing them and planning for them will help your change initiative be more successful. As Proverbs 15:22 states, "Plans fail with no counsel, but with many counselors they succeed." Let wisdom about how the brain works serve as one of your counselors.

Organize Your Thoughts around a Brain-Friendly Buy-In Plan

The actual logistics of change are certainly important. But it's equally important to develop a specific plan to bring your team along. You don't want to force the change but to encourage the team to buy into it. So the "O" of *ROPES* involves *organizing a buy-in plan* with the brain in mind even before you begin the change. The more brain-friendly insights you incorporate early on, the better you can prepare your team to successfully navigate the change.

Here are several brain-friendly guidelines around which to design your plan.

Step into Their Shoes

Neuroscientists have learned that often what we say we will do we don't, and what we say we won't do, we often do. Of course it doesn't take a brain scientist to figure that out. But they've also discovered that when the brain's *Accountant* lights up (Falk et al., 2010), it can accurately predict future behavior. This part of the brain gives us the ability to see another's perspective by intentionally stepping inside his or her shoes (Zaki & Ochsner, 2012). It's called *mentalizing*. As we think about ourselves or think about others, we engage our *Accountant*. And what we do in the future is correlated with that part of the brain lighting up. So when your team takes your perspective and when you take theirs, you can help move the change forward.

So as you begin to create your plan, think about how you can step into your team's shoes. Try to discern their perspective of the pending change by asking yourself questions like these:

- What are their concerns?
- How do they feel about this change?
- What do they fear?
- What do they think is going on inside your head?
- What might be their biggest objections?

Better yet, ask a few key people for their perspective. Also ask yourself how you can create an environment so your team will feel safe to discuss the change. Feeling safe can create a toward response that will make your team more open to change (Whiting et al., 2012). Take a moment and write down your own thoughts about how others may view the change.

Envision the Benefits

When we imagine accomplishing something, we activate the same brain circuits as if we actually performed the task (Knäuper et al., 2009; Munzert et al., 2008). As you create your plan, include ways to help your team envision the positive benefits the change can bring. Using the illustration from earlier about a new service, here's how a leader might help his or her team see how that change will benefit them: Help the team envision how creating a new service will provide opportunities to develop more volunteers that can reduce the load they currently carry. Consider providing compensation time when the added hours come into play. Help them see how another service option can reach more people, thus bring them joy at seeing changed lives.

Break into manageable bites their fears and concerns you've discerned by stepping into their shoes. Address each one. Fill in their knowledge gaps with information that creates a compelling image of the future. Replace those gaps with faith messages that with God's help you can make the change. Encourage your team with Hebrews 11:1: "Faith is the reality of what we hope for, the proof of what we don't see."

Finally, the more you communicate that the change is less about you and your interests and more about their needs, the better your change will stick (Stiff & Mongeau, 2002, p. 111).

Write down the benefits from your team's perspective here.

Manage Expectations

As you create your buy-in plan, consider the power of expectations. The brain likes to know what to expect so it can prepare for and anticipate what's coming. If your team feels uncertain about the future, their anxiety will rise because that uncertainty can create an away state. One way to help moderate this anxiety is to plan how you will set expectations.

It's wise to set realistic ones and to avoid overselling the benefits. Yet still build in hopeful expectations. When we expect something good, we get a dopamine boost. It's like the placebo effect when people think they are taking a real drug for a health issue, even though it may be a sugar pill. The sugar pill actually helps some people feel better because their positive expectations activated a part of the brain that tempers pain (Fournier et al., 2010). And positive expectations prime our brains to be even more receptive. David Rock wrote, "What you expect is what you experience" (Rock, 2009, p. 140). So when you implement the change, you want to have met the expectations you communicated. Better yet, exceed them. Our brains love it when we get something unexpected, like exceeded expectations.

When your team experiences the positive benefits of change, their dopamine levels increase, which puts them in a better mood. And when our teams are in better moods, they can engender more confidence in your leadership. They then become even more open to new experiences and change. One way to engender this confidence is to recognize and celebrate small wins along the way (more about that shortly). The scriptures even tell us to do this when it says we are to rejoice with others who rejoice (Rom 12:15).

What positive benefits can you plan to communicate?

Invite Input

A buy-in plan implies that you will intentionally help people own the change. Why should they own it? Because people don't like being told what to do (i.e., "You need to change"). They would rather come up with their own ideas. Within reason, provide your team with significant opportunities to give input into how the change will look. Give away small components of change to those lower on the leadership organizational chart. Although your key leadership must decide the *what* of change, provide options and opportunities for your entire team to fashion the *how*. Remember, the brain loves freedom and autonomy. In the next chapter I explain in detail a related concept: how to foster insight in your team.

Also give your team real, tangible, and easy channels through which they can give you feedback about the change. Simply knowing that you are serious about listening will decrease your team's threat response and fear about the change.

What mechanism can you set up to solicit input from your team?

Seed Your Culture with a Change Mentality

As I've often written, change evokes fear in our emotional centers because it implies threat, and the brain is wired to avoid threat and danger. However, the more familiar something becomes to us, the less threatening it will appear to us. So the more you familiarize your team with change, especially *before* you initiate a major one, the more likely they will receive it.

How can you do that?

First, begin with your key leadership. Incorporate a change mentality into your leadership culture so that your core team or influencers don't see it as a threat. Regularly include conversations about change in staff meetings, retreats, and leadership training. Encourage your leaders to think about it. Make change management a core competency you expect from your staff. Hire staff and recruit key volunteers who aren't averse to change. Seek to make the concept less foreign.

Second, include some aspect of change into your annual plans. Make it a core component in every planning cycle, not just when you need to make significant changes. Keep the conversation about change on the front burner. Help leaders think about ways to stay ahead of change rather than reacting to it when change becomes necessary.

Finally, often teach about the biblical basis of change. Share stories of great heroes of the faith who embraced change and furthered the Kingdom as a result. Abraham obeyed God and moved to a foreign land. God blessed him with a new nation. Ruth left her home, family, and nation to follow Naomi into a strange land. As a result, she became part of the lineage of Jesus. And the disciples gave up their jobs to follow Jesus as his disciples. They were responsible for spreading the gospel after Jesus ascended to heaven. Remember, stories move and motivate.

What are you currently doing or what specifically can you begin to do to seed a change mentality into your organization's culture and teams?

Persuade with Brain-Friendly Messaging

Liberally sprinkle these concepts into your communication plan leading up to, during, and after the change. Communicate these more often than what you may think is necessary. You've thought about the change much more than your team has. So what may seem redundant to you may not seem so to them.

Help Your Team See the Progress They've Already Made

The more motivated we feel, the more readily we embrace change. We feel motivated when the neurotransmitter dopamine increases in our brains. And when we experience positive events in life, dopamine increases. Communicating and celebrating small wins through the change process can help gain buy-in from others by helping them experience a feel-good surge of dopamine. Each win can give your team a boost of motivation to continue to move forward with the change. One study illustrates this concept in action.

Patrons at a particular car wash received vouchers that gave them a free car wash after eight visits (Nunes & Dreze, 2006). But the vouchers differed in a significant way. Some received vouchers that required all eight circles to be marked after each subsequent visit. The rest received vouchers that required ten circles to be marked, but two of them were already marked. So both actually required the same number of visits, but one appeared to include freebies from the car wash.

Guess which group returned most often to fulfill the required eight visits for the free wash? The ones whose voucher showed two circles already marked. The offer was framed as a partial win, and the brain loves to win. Since the patrons felt that they were already 20 percent there, they figured, "Why not finish it out?" The ten-circle voucher communicated that the car wash owners were giving away something free up front, a benefit to the customer. They experienced it as win that helped motivate them to keep coming back for another win, a free car wash. Similarly, when we communicate progress through wins, even small ones, it can motivate your team to continue to face the challenges the change will bring.

Help People Act as If

When we're given the option between choices, studies show that once we choose one, the choice we made seems more appealing than it originally did. And the choice we didn't make seems less appealing (Sharot et al., 2009). Our commitment to the choice, once made, increases. In other words, feeling follows action. When we behave as if (by faith we move toward the change) our brain likes the change more. I once heard Rick Warren, the author of *The Purpose Driven Life*, say that when he needed to do something he wasn't particularly motivated to do, he'd tell himself, "I'll give it ten minutes." When he did that, the motivation soon followed.

However, the key to *acting as if* lies in personal choice. A person has to willingly choose to make the decision. One way you could apply this concept is to encourage your team to take small steps toward the change without feeling like they have to swallow the whole thing at once. Once they take those steps and find that their choices weren't as scary as they thought, it can motivate them to take bigger faith-stretching steps. Acting as if is like a muscle. The more you do it, the stronger you get at it.

Frame Your Change with Your Audience in Mind

Avoidance or Approach?

How we frame the change is crucial. We can frame our change (our goals) in two ways: approach focused or avoidance focused. An avoidance goal is one that we frame as, "We need to do this (the change) or else this (bad thing) will happen." An avoidance goal seeks to avoid something bad. Thus when we avoid the thing, we feel relieved. We'd frame an approach goal, however, as, "We need to do this (the change) so that we can have or experience this (the benefit)." The motivation to change is to experience something better rather than avoid something bad. When we experience the benefit, we feel good. Approach goals focus toward getting a reward and avoidance goals upon avoiding something negative. The following example explains this concept and how these two kinds of goals motivate different personalities.

In this study, participants were evaluated to see how they would respond to messages to floss more (Sherman et al., 2006). Those motivated more by avoidance goals flossed more over the duration of the study when they read articles that described how flossing helps *avoid* such problems as bad breath and gum disease. However, those motivated more by approach goals flossed more often after they read articles about the *benefits* of flossing, like healthy gums and good breath.

Simply put, our brains process motivation differently. Left-brain-leaning people tend to be motivated more by approach goals and right-brain-leaning people more by avoidance goals (Pizzagalli et al., 2005; Berkman, 2012). So the better you know your team, the better you can frame your change. And since your team probably includes both kinds of "brains," framing the change with both an avoidance and an approach mind-set can help you connect with both groups.

Motivation or Instruction?

Another concept to consider as you persuade involves the kind of information your team needs. Some people need answers about the *how* of change (concrete actions) (Cross et al., 2009), while others need answers about the *why* of change (abstract motivations) (Desmurget & Sirigu, 2009). And our brains can't be in both the *why* and *how* modes at the same time. When we think about the *how*, thinking about the *why* is minimized, and vice versa. Leaders tend to live in the *why* because we think about long-term implications of our decisions. However, front-line people, like middle managers and engineers, tend to live more in the *how*. So again, since both of these kinds of people are probably on your team, design your communication strategies with both in mind. Some will need more motivation and some will need more information.

> What's the makeup of your team: avoidance or approach, motivation or instruction?

Personally Connect to Your Audience

I've often heard this old saying: *People don't care how much you know until they know how much you care.* The saying has sound neuroscience roots. Genuineness and a warm, caring style can endear your team to you and the change. Empathy, the ability to see through another's eyes (stepping into their shoes, as we discussed earlier), is crucial to helping your team embrace your change. Alfred Adler, the famous psychologist, gives us one of the best definitions of empathy: "to see with the eyes of another, to hear with the ears of another, to feel with the heart of another" (Chalquist, n.d.). When you communicate empathy, seek to build relational rapport by connecting at more than a superficial level. In fact, one study showed the pragmatic value of empathy. Empathetic doctors were sued less than those not considered empathetic (Ambady, 2002). Perhaps more empathy from leaders could decrease conflict in the workplace.

One way you can connect and build empathy is to share mistakes you've made through the change process. All leaders make them and should learn through them and share what they've learned. Unfortunately, some leadership cultures discourage this type of openness. We don't want to look like failures or appear weak. Yet mistake sharing can benefit others. Brain studies show that when we observe how a friend learned from his mistake, we learn from it just as if we ourselves made the same mistake (Kang et al., 2010). And these studies discovered that when a friend sees a mistake another friend made, he views the mistake as if it were his own mistake.

However, our teams can't learn from our mistakes if we never share them. So the more you share your mistakes with your team (within reason), the more they will personally connect to you, learn from you, and follow you. Humility, an important character quality, comes into play here. For Jesus himself said, "He has pulled the powerful down from their thrones and lifted up the lowly" (Luke 1:52).

Repeat the Common Why Often and Delegate the How

Leaders must constantly answer two key questions, especially during change: "Why are we making this change?" and "How do we do it?" A shared *why* can help teams avoid silos and increase personal productivity (Shteynberg & Galinsky, 2011). Leaders should prioritize vision clarity as one of their top two roles along with leadership development. When you share a clear *why* and allow your teams to create the *how*, you'll foster an atmosphere of personal freedom and autonomy, a key component for high-performing teams (Rock & Cox, 2012).

Delegating the how also encourages your teams to create their own solutions. And when they solve problems with their own insights, their brains change so that they remember and own those solutions better (Ludmer et al., 2011). Plus, insight gives a nice burst of dopamine and energy, which motivate teams more than when a leader simply gives answers. When you give your team the freedom to implement the *why* by letting them determine the *how*, you again foster the key components of high-performing teams, freedom and autonomy, which boosts buy-in (Rock & Cox, 2012).

Evaluate Progress through Brain-Friendly Feedback

Leaders most often skip or gloss over a crucial step in the change process, evaluation and feedback during and after the change. Often they're glad to have made the change and still be standing, yet fail to reflect on what they learned or if the change really worked. It's much easier to move to a new project than to take time to reflect over the previous one. This neglect happens at both the organizational and the personal levels. I've performed many annual performance reviews hoping to create change in a staff person, but in retrospect I question if that type of feedback really resulted in lasting change.

My concerns were confirmed when I learned that one extensive study showed that up to 70 percent of feedback has either no or negative impact (Kluger & DeNisi, 1996). Unfortunately, for decades business has assumed that feedback improves performance. That assumption was based on decades-old studies that indicated that traditionally given feedback improved performance. Since then, leaders have assumed that the traditional annual performance reviews help improve performance. However, those studies primarily focused on motor skill performance, like threading bolts into nuts or shooting arrows into targets (DeNisi & Kluger, 2000). Most of today's organizations' teams require much more intensive thinking skills.

In the next chapter I delve more deeply into personal performance reviews and feedback. However, at the organizational level, effective change is not complete until it's been evaluated. Consider incorporating these four suggestions to effectively evaluate your change.

🧠 *Keep People Informed about Your Progress and Welcome Their Input*

Build into your buy-in plan specific dates when you will communicate progress. Tell your team how you will evaluate progress and when you will report it. Bring all your key players into the conversation. If they feel they are in the "out" group, resistance to change will be higher, as it creates an away response (Rock & Cox, 2012). Be thorough in your assessments. If the change is not going as planned, be honest yet focus on solutions, not problems. Give hope.

Elicit feedback from several sources, not just from those at the top of your organizational chart. The more collaborative your evaluation process, the more successful the change (London & Smither, 1995). When others feel that they contributed to the evaluation process, they sense more freedom and thus more ownership.

🧠 *Continue to Acknowledge That Change Is Scary*

When you talk about the progress you're making, continue to verbalize that you understand how difficult and scary change can be. Be sure that you don't speak in a patronizing way that implies that it's difficult for your team and not for you. Let them know that it's scary for you as well, another way to build empathy. Help your team realize that it's normal to feel unsettled during change and that it will pass.

🧠 *Tell Stories of People Who Are Navigating the Change Well*

Narrative persuasion is a technique that uses indirect communication through story and example. Often we try to persuade others with a direct approach that communicates just the facts, like, "We are going to make a change, and here are the reasons why." The direct approach often is not effective. Neuroscientists have confirmed common sense that storytelling has a powerful effect on behavior (Falk et al., 2012). Storytelling helps others "see" through the eyes of another. And when that happens it engages our brain's *Accountant*, which can predict future behavior (Falk et al., 2012). As you solicit feedback, look for stories of people who are managing the change well. Tell their stories as you give updates about your progress. When your team members can see successful responses to change through stories of others, it will help them navigate the change better.

🧠 *Stay Reasonably Connected to Your Biggest Resisters*

In my book *People-Pleasing Pastors: Avoiding the Pitfalls of Approval-Motivated Leadership* (Stone, 2014), I devote an entire chapter to explaining why we need to stay connected to our critics. Change will bring detractors to the surface, as the Bible often shows. When Moses sent Joshua and the spies to scout out the promised land, even though they returned with glowing reports about the opportunity before them, many people resisted the change by spreading a bad report (Num 13:32). Stay connected to your detractors, but don't become their punching bag. Rather, if you stay calmly connected to them, you can help calm their emotionality and mitigate their opposition. Keeping them in the dark or cutting them off will simply intensify their opposition.

So, we've seen in this chapter that good leaders know how to wisely manage change. I believe that if you apply the neuroscience insights reflected in the *ROPE* model, your change initiatives can go more smoothly.

> 🧠 *Recognize* why the brain resists change.

> 🧠 *Organize* your thoughts around a brain-friendly buy-in plan.

> 🧠 *Persuade* with brain-friendly messaging.

> 🧠 *Evaluate* progress through brain-friendly feedback.

In the next chapter I will discuss how neuroscience insight impacts several other areas crucial to leadership:

- increasing creativity in your team
- giving effective performance reviews
- making brainstorming work

The science behind...*Brain Surprise 9*: *If you're feeling rejected, your brain can make you feel better if you take two Tylenol tablets. (Dewall et al., 2010)*

We experience physical pain in some of the same brain regions we experience social pain, like rejection. Our *Accountant* and part of our insula are both involved in registering physical and social pain. In one study participants were divided into two groups. Over a period of three weeks, one group took Tylenol daily, and the other group took a placebo. In follow-up fMRI studies, the social pain regions of the brains of those who took Tylenol lit up less than those who took placebos. So the saying, "Sticks and stones may break my bones, but words will never hurt me" is dead wrong.

Chapter 10

Three Brain-Friendly Skills Easily Overlooked

Brain Surprise 10: *If you need a boost of motivation, simply thinking about chocolate might help.*

———

Thus far I've unpacked acronyms that describe four essential leadership domains that brain insight can help us improve, two in the self-leadership category and two in the team leadership category. With the Holy Spirit's help, we'll become better leaders when we learn to control our emotions, improve our personal productivity, grow teams, and manage change well. These four domains certainly don't cover every leadership competency. It would take volumes to cover every area. However, I felt that three other areas warranted a combined chapter: brainstorming and creativity, giving answers to your team rather than fostering their insight, and feedback/performance reviews.

As a Christian leader, I believe that God gives each of us unique gifts and talents that he wants us to use for his purposes and glory. And the more we're able to incorporate God's truth, whether it comes from God's word or from really smart people who know a lot about the brain, the more God is honored. So in addition to the four domains I've already discussed, consider these next three areas through a Christian worldview and consider how they might enhance your pastoral or marketplace leadership.

Brainstorming and Creativity

Alex Osborne published a book in 1948 called *Your Creative Power* in which he described the creative secrets he had learned from his advertising agency, B.B.D.O., one of the most successful at the time. His most-often used idea was brainstorming. He believed that the best way to generate ideas was to attack the same objective to find multiple solutions. Two key assumptions set apart brainstorming from other group activities: go for quantity instead of quality ideas, and don't allow anyone in the brainstorming session to criticize the ideas. He believed that if people worried that others might criticize their ideas, the process wouldn't work. Fear of criticism would stifle people from offering their ideas and decrease their number, or so he thought.

Brainstorming is now one of today's most widely used creative tools. The problem is this: It doesn't work, at least in the way it's usually used. It actually stifles creativity, and many studies since Osborne's book have proved it. The first study was performed at Yale University in 1958 (Taylor et al., 1958). It involved forty-eight male undergraduates divided into twelve brainstorming groups who were given a series of creative puzzles to solve. The study also included a control group of another forty-eight students given the same puzzles to solve. The results? The individual students created twice as many solutions as the solutions from the brainstorming groups.

So if traditional brainstorming falls short, what's the best way to generate ideas? Should you totally eliminate these sessions? No. But if you change the rules to allow appropriate criticism and debate, your creative sessions can yield greater results, as one researcher discovered. Charlan Nemeth, a psychology professor at the University of California–Berkley, performed a creativity study in 2003 (Nemeth et al., 2004). She divided 265 female students into groups of five and asked them to generate as many ideas as possible on how to decrease traffic congestion in the San Francisco Bay area. Each team received one of three conditions and was given twenty minutes to complete the task. Either they used the traditional "no criticism" brainstorming technique, or they generated as many ideas as possible but could debate and criticize each one, or they received no instructions. The "debate and criticize" teams generated 20 percent more ideas than the other two groups.

So if you want to increase the number of ideas, encourage your teams to generate as many ideas as possible, but don't stop there. As they generate ideas, encourage them to debate and criticize them, all with the right spirit, of course. When you do this, you create greater mental engagement and force team members to reassess their own ideas, which results in more ideas. Debate also adds the element of surprise that engages the brain.

Two other ideas can add to your team's creativity. One study on what made Broadway musicals successful found that creative teams that included both familiar people and newbies produced the most successful musicals (Ellenberg, 2012). Another study done on scientists themselves discovered that the best quality papers came from scientists whose offices or labs were relatively close to each other, less than ten meters apart (Ruder, 2011). In fact, one of the most famous legends of innovation, a building called Building 20 at MIT, gave us radar, microwaves, and the first video game. Scientists were haphazardly crammed into this old building, and its design forced solitary-minded scientists to mix and mingle. Their chance meetings spurred conversations and innovation.

So consider these tips to help improve your team's creativity:

- When you brainstorm, encourage debate, dissent, and healthy criticism of ideas. Set these rules beforehand, though, to keep the debate healthy and avoid an away response.
    o Don't personally attack people.
    o Use such phrases as, "I have a different view," "I see things differently," or "What about this?"
    o Reiterate the other person's viewpoint before offering your own.
    o Clarify the other person's viewpoint first.
- Keep your creative teams diverse. Include new people and women and men.
- Make sure the brainstorming leader is affirming and not overbearing and that he or she doesn't unintentionally drive a personal agenda.
- Create spaces in your office that encourage frequent and spontaneous interactions.
- Don't allow one person to dominate brainstorming sessions. Sometimes a "know-it-all" can shut down creativity.

- Be observant of something called "social loafing," our tendency to feel less responsible for a project in a group than when doing a project alone. Some on your team may sit back and let the rest of the team generate the ideas. Guard against that. Studies with a rope tug-of-war showed that blindfolded people who believed they were pulling a rope alone pulled 18 percent harder than those who thought they were on a team (Karau & Hart, 1998). However, the more cohesive the group, the less social loafing there is.

- When beginning a creative session, the leader should acknowledge that everyone is on equal footing and that he or she wants everyone to feel that they can contribute.

- Before your brainstorming session, ask the team members to generate ideas on their own and to submit them in writing before the session. Sharing that list as you begin will foster even more ideas.

- Be wary of too much group harmony in creative sessions. Artificial harmony that fosters a "too nice" atmosphere can stifle appraisal of alternatives.

- When trying to solve a problem in a brainstorming session, challenge the group to present counterintuitive solutions (i.e., what's obviously not the solution to the problem). This approach can foster even more creativity.

- Provide an incubation period to let ideas simmer. If you give the team a brain break and encourage daydreaming, when they come back to the problem, solutions often arise (Sio & Ormerod, 2009). Sometimes ideas come to us while doing something moderately taxing and daydreaming at the same time (e.g., taking a shower or walking on a treadmill). It's called unconscious thought theory, or UTT (Dijksterhuis & Nordgren, 2006). UTT proposes that solutions to complex problems often come when we are not intentionally trying to solve them.

- When trying to solve problems, encourage your team to imagine themselves a year from now instead of imagining themselves tomorrow. Studies show that this time perspective fosters more creativity (Förster et al., 2004).

166

Giving Answers vs. Fostering Insight

Wise leaders encourage their teams to solve their problems with their own insight rather than with the leader's insight. When a staff person or a volunteer brings a problem to us, it's often easier and less time-consuming to give them advice and solve their problem. Yet in the long run such a response can foster dependency on us to solve their problems and diminish their motivation simply because the solution isn't theirs. And people are less likely to act on somebody else's ideas anyway. So how can we replace "answer giving" with self-generated insight?

Although related to brainstorming and creativity as discussed earlier, fostering individual insight deserves its own explanation. Insight is a solution to a problem that recombines what we know in a new and fresh way that often leads to creativity. Rather than solving a problem analytically, when we turn our attention outwardly on the problem, insight occurs when we turn our attention inward and become less focused on the problem. This inward focus can help us experience a sudden "aha" solution. This historical illustration about insight describes the "aha" process well.

We use the word *eureka*, attributed to Archimedes (c. 287–c. 212 BCE), to describe an "aha" moment, a flash of insight we sometimes get. As a brilliant scientist in antiquity, Archimedes is perhaps most known for a story about his inventing a method to determine an object's volume. A goldsmith had forged a crown of gold for the then king, King Hiero II. He was concerned, however, that the goldsmith had substituted the cheaper metal, silver, for some of the gold. He asked Archimedes to find the truth without melting the crown. This stumped Archimedes until a flash of insight appeared to him.

As the famous story goes, one day as he took a bath, he noticed the water level rise as he stepped in. Suddenly he realized that by making a few mathematical calculations, he could use water volume displacement of the crown to determine if it was indeed made of pure gold. In his excitement, he ran into the streets naked, crying, "Eureka, Eureka!" which means in Greek, "I have found it." Thus, we use the word *eureka* for insight. Through this insight he then discovered that the goldsmith had indeed substituted silver for some of the crown's gold. I'm sure the king's *Panic Alarm* went off when he heard the news (and the goldsmith's when he got caught). Archimedes had discovered an insight in a moment when he wasn't even thinking about the problem. When we get a "eureka" or an "aha" insight, we just know the answer without actually knowing how we got it. The insight doesn't come piece by piece, but usually all at once.

Researchers who study insight use a word game called Compound Remote Associate (CRA) problems. Study participants try to create three two-word phrases from three words that could share a common word. For example, consider these three words: *barrel, root,* and *belly*. What two-word phrases can you create that share a common word? Participants often use the word *beer* to create *beer barrel, root beer,* and *beer belly*. After they solve the problem, they press a button to indicate how they solved it, either logically or with an "aha" insight. Using both EEG and fMRI, neuroscientists then examine their brain functioning to learn what happens during insight (Jung-Beeman et al., 2008).

Through these studies they've discovered a process that occurs in our brain when it receives an insight. First, our brain is at rest in the default mode. We may be daydreaming or our minds may be wandering. MRI studies show that at this stage, the alpha wave (the wave active when the brain idles during daydreaming and relaxation) spikes. This indicates that our brain is visually gating (Sandkühler & Bhattacharya, 2008), reducing the visual input it's processing to reduce distractions. This is in contrast to the brain's dominant wave, the beta wave, which is active during visual focus and alertness. The alpha wave shows that our *Error Detector* is more active prior to an insight. This makes us more aware of competing alternatives and enhances our predisposition to switch between different solutions (Beeman, n.d.), potentially creating an insight. That is, if one solution doesn't work, the brain will try another. Our *Error Detector* helps orchestrate attention since it is so highly connected to the rest of the brain.

Finally, at the moment an insight occurs, the gamma wave spikes (Kounios et al., 2006). You'll recall that the gamma wave, the fastest brain wave, sweeps across the entire brain forty times per second to bring our brain to attention, much like how a conductor synchronizes an orchestra when he raises his baton. The gamma band activity indicates new brain maps are being formed, the insight. And when that happens it literally feels good because neurotransmitters are released. As the insight occurs at the point of gamma synchrony, right hemisphere activity also increases to help us make connections with subtle associations we might have otherwise missed. The brain's right hemisphere, which processes information more intuitively and holistically, apparently drives the insight process.

I envision a setting ripe for insight akin to a guy drinking lemonade while sunning in a lounge chair at the beach. Then, as he reads a fishing magazine, the solution to a nagging work problem suddenly pops into his mind. That image contrasts to his intense mental state a week prior at work when he tried to solve the problem, much like what Rodin's famous sculpture *The Thinker* pictures. So insights are more apt to come when our brains are less focused and more rested.

Consider these tips to help your team learn to develop insight:

- **Daydreaming:** Insight often comes when we daydream and allow our minds to wander (Christoff et al., 2009). Teach your team how daydreaming can help them solve problems. Encourage your team to schedule times to daydream and to allow their minds to wander rather than always actively trying to solve problems. Help them realize that thinking less about a problem may actually bring about the solution. In fact, some companies, such as Google, Intuit, and Twitter, expect their employees to take time for daydreaming about projects other that than those they're working on (Waytz & Mason, 2013). Of course, analytical process solving or a mixture of analytical and daydreaming might make more sense in some situations.

- **Mood:** When we are in a positive mood, problem solving often comes more easily (Subramaniam et al., 2008). Yet when we're anxious, we solve fewer problems because the anxiety uses up brain resources. So if you're facing a dilemma in your organization, it might help if the team watched a funny movie to stir the creative juices.

- **Location:** Encourage your team to discover the kinds of activities that help put them into an insight state. Two settings have helped me generate insight. Ideas pop into my mind when I read and walk at a reasonable pace on my treadmill. Insight also comes more readily when our family leaves for vacation while it's still dark. I'm the driver, and I'm usually the only one awake that early in the morning. With little roadside distraction, my brain has generated many good ideas during those three or four hours of solitude.

- **Application:** Although insight gives us a nice dopamine rush, we all know that the feeling eventually wears off. Remind your team to record their insights in an easy-to-remember location so that they won't forget them. Even if your team member can't immediately act on an insight, getting him or her to commit to acting on it at a later time can help translate the insight into action (Rock, 2007, p. 108).

- **Speed:** If you're working with team members who are trying to find a solution to a problem, don't rush the process. Give them time to engage their brains. Allow space in conversations, and encourage those team members to carve out some down time to give their brains a break.

- **Pattern:** In David Rock's book, *Quiet Leadership*, he recommends a four-step process to help foster insight. He calls it the "dance of insight." I've summarized it here (Rock, 2007, pp. 111–50).
    - Permission: ask permission to have a conversation with another about an issue or to go deeper on an issue before launching into it (without necessarily using the word *permission*).
    - Placement: clearly explain these components of a conversation: what it will be about, what's going to happen in it, what you hope to accomplish by it, and what you'd like the other person to do during the conversation. In other words, placement answers these questions: why, when, how, and who?
    - Questioning: learn to use powerful questions to encourage your team members to do their own thinking rather than offering them advice. Focus questions more on solutions and less on problems and details. In this stage you're helping them focus on their own thinking.
    - Clarifying: clarify the answers team members give to your questions to help them verbalize what they are not saying that they should be saying. Clarifying can help them realize what's behind their words. Although a form of paraphrasing, clarifying is a higher level of conversation.

Rock captures the "dance of insight" this way:

It's about getting permission before getting personal, then making sure you're both on the same page before asking a question, then asking questions that create new maps in people's minds. As you quietly facilitate this dance, you'll see people's faces changing as they move from the awareness of a dilemma, to reflecting, to having illumination, and then being ready to take action. (Rock, 2007, p. 150)

Feedback and Performance Reviews

We naturally resist feedback because we don't like somebody else trying to change us. However, change is the essence of sanctification, how the Holy Spirit forms us into Christ's image. And the book of Proverbs often uses the word "fool" for someone who resists change and counsel from others. Yet, even for Christians feedback often feels threatening.

In the previous chapter I referred to a study that discovered that giving feedback through performance reviews often doesn't work. In that study the researchers discovered that only 30 percent of the time did performance reviews improve performance (Kluger & DeNisi, 1996). Not only do most performance reviews fail to yield results, but also they may actually diminish the self-esteem of those we evaluate, as this study reflected.

One study involved a simple experiment on college students. The students first held a mock interview. Afterwards, as they lay in an MRI machine, they received evaluations on their performance through forty-five separate evaluative words given by someone who observed their interview. The words were equally divided into fifteen neutral ones, fifteen positive ones, and fifteen negative ones. Even though the positive and neutral words outweighed the negative ones two to one, over 40 percent of the students experienced lower self-esteem. And the part of the brain that experiences rejection from others lit up in the scanner (Eisenberger et al., 2011).

I understand this insight through personal experience. Years ago a key leader in a church I led repeatedly told me that although I possessed great character, my teaching didn't connect with the people's hearts nor did I have sufficient leadership skills to bring the church to the next level. He assumed that his positives outweighed the negative. They didn't. My self-esteem suffered a blow, and after reading this study, I now understand why I felt so discouraged after his comments.

So if feedback potentially hinders performance rather than helps, should we eliminate it? No. We need feedback, and so do our teams, so that we all can grow. I believe that if you redesign your feedback process by incorporating some simple changes, you can make your feedback and performance evaluations effective. As you evaluate your process and incorporate the ten "C"s of a good feedback system that I list in the next section, first consider these six foundational thoughts:

1. The traditional "sandwich" technique usually doesn't work. This technique sandwiches the negative between two positives. If you've ever experienced such feedback from someone, you probably only remembered the negative one and not the positive ones.

2. We usually experience traditional feedback as an away response rather than a toward response because it feels threatening. That is, such feedback often triggers our *Panic Alarm*, which evokes fear and defensiveness. This causes our *CEO* to go offline, and we can miss the benefits from the feedback.

3. Feedback often unintentionally focuses on the person's identity, who they are, rather than on the behavior or their tasks. When that happens, we feel threatened and hear little else.

4. Most feedback systems are based on one-off annual reviews. Such feedback rarely sticks and often creates employee stress that reduces productivity leading up to and following the reviews.

5. Response to the gaps given through feedback can result in any of these four behaviors in the reviewee: change of behavior, change of goals, rejection of the feedback, or simply avoidance of others or the tasks (Smither & Walker, 2004).

6. Reviewees usually pay more attention to qualitative feedback (narrative comments) than they do to quantitative evaluations (Smither & Walker, 2004).

I've categorized the ten "C"s into two categories. One category directly relates to the *person* who's receiving or giving a review. The second category, the process, relates to issues about the process itself.

The Person

- **Community:** The person receiving the review ideally should feel relationally connected to the reviewer (Ibarra, 1999). When a reviewee has a relationship with the reviewer, he's more likely to receive the feedback (Dixon et al., 2010). When the reviewee feels threatened, though, the feedback is more likely to be ignored. Proverbs 27:6 illustrates this idea: "Trustworthy are the bruises of a friend; excessive are the kisses of an enemy." If you are the leader, try to forge a relationship before giving feedback.

- **Coachability:** Help the reviewees be coachable. Help them see the value of the review process (Atwater & Brett, 2005). The more open they are to changing, the more likely they will actually change and grow from feedback.

- **Connected to their goals:** The reviewees must connect feedback they receive to how they see themselves in the future (Kluger & DeNisi, 1996) and to their larger goals (Ashford et al., 2003). We more easily receive feedback when it's connected to our future goals. In the feedback process, help the reviewees get a picture of how they can become better leaders, pastors, volunteers, board members, or staff persons through the feedback process. Give them a vision of the future by connecting the proposed changes to their goals. Help them connect the change to how it can positively affect them by improving their performance. Perhaps a better term would be *feed-forward* (Koen et al., 2012) instead of *feedback*.

- **Content versus person focused (DeNisi & Kluger, 2000):** Since the brain has five times more negative networks than positive ones (Baumeister et al., 2001), feedback should focus on the problem and the behavior rather than on a person's personal defects (Dixon, 2013). And rather than dissecting the problem, focus on potential solutions that solve the problem or improve performance. When we focus on the content rather than the person, we can take the emotional charge out of the conversation and the potential status threat. When we feel socially threatened, our brain's *Panic Alarm* engages just as if we faced an actual physical threat.

173

The Process

- **Credible:** The reviewee must see the reviewer as unbiased and informed (Waldman et al., 1998). Get your facts straight before giving feedback.

- **Clarify through self-feedback:** The most effective feedback often comes through the reviewees first evaluating themselves. I've usually begun my reviews with a self-evaluation assessment tool the team members complete on themselves before the interview. This provides good talking points and an entrée into discussing other topics. In addition, when reviewees feel as if they contributed to the feedback process, they'll sense greater control and more autonomy, which can help put them into a toward state.

- **Coaching:** Although similar to coachability, coaching involves you as the leader. Include as part of the feedback process follow-up through coaching. After a review, provide a written summary to the reviewee that outlines the specific behaviors and tasks you want the team member to do. Phil Dixon, an expert on feedback systems, has concisely captured the importance of coaching follow-up with this statement: "Feedback without follow up is futile" (Dixon, 2013). This step, perhaps more than any other, will make the greatest difference in how well feedback will effect change. Coaching will reinforce and spur progress.

- **Closeness:** Feedback is best given in close proximity to the time a team member does something that needs correcting or changing (Dixon et al., 2010). Don't wait until the formal evaluation cycle to give feedback. Real-time feedback yields the best results.

- **Collaborative:** The process ideally includes peers and superiors (London & Smither, 1995). Three hundred sixty degree reviews, when incorporated with the other "C"s, can add great value to the feedback process. However, be sure to clearly explain to your team member how such reviews work. I once did a 360 degree review and didn't sufficiently prepare the team member for how it would be used. It did more harm than good.

- **Culture infused:** Use feedback regularly as an ongoing experience for your team. If you infuse it into your culture as a positive and helpful developmental tool, it won't seem as foreign to your team as the traditional annual review often feels. One way to do this is to regularly teach about its value, especially before formal reviews begin. When you teach, remind your team that we all may feel uncomfortable with feedback but that such discomfort can help us grow and become more productive. Cueing up your team in this way will bring more certainty and moderate an away response.

In this chapter we looked at three other brain-friendly, moment-in-time skills: brainstorming, fostering insight, and feedback. Consider applying these insights in advance of brainstorming, as your team asks you for advice, and before you give feedback. Incorporating even some of these small changes can bring significant results.

The science behind... *Brain Surprise 10*: *If you need a boost of motivation, simply thinking about chocolate might help. (Georgia Health Sciences, 2011)*

Most people love chocolate. Although the benefits of chocolate in moderation, especially dark chocolate, have been touted for years, recent research has shown the brain benefits. One researcher says that eating chocolate, or just the thought of doing so, can stir a mild production of dopamine, the reward and motivation neurotransmitter. So the next time you need a bit of an emotional or motivational boost, and don't want additional calories, daydreaming about chocolate may do the trick, at least for a few minutes.

Section IV

Going Forward

Chapter 11

Final Thoughts

Brain Surprise 11: *Simply changing your posture could brighten your day.*

In chapter 2 I shared about our journey with my daughter Tiffany as we struggled to find treatment for her brain tumor. In many ways, that excruciating experience forced me to begin to look at my own life and leadership and ask myself if brain insight might offer answers to perplexing questions that often bugged me. It had helped our family so much; perhaps it could also help me build significant ministry. Although my learning journey is far from over, I'm convinced that Christian leaders will do well to stay abreast of how brain insight positively impacts life and leadership.

In my daily quiet time I often read the devotional by Oswald Chambers, *My Utmost for His Highest.* In the updated version, he writes this for May 20:

> When a person is born again, there is a period of time when he does not have the same vitality in his thinking or reasoning that he previously had. We must learn to express this new life within us, which comes by forming the mind of Christ (see Philippians 2.5). Luke 21.19 (By your patience possess your souls) means that we take possession of our souls through patience. But many of us prefer to stay at the entrance to the Christian life, instead of going on to create and build our soul in accordance with the new life God has placed within us. We fail because we are ignorant of the way God has made us, and we blame things on the devil that are actually the result of our own undisciplined natures. Just think what we could be when we are awakened to the truth! (Chambers, 1992)

When I read that day's devotional, several phrases rung true for me.

- "Forming the mind of Christ" and everything that concept implies for my spiritual life, my leadership, and how my mind and brain works takes patience. I've often lacked it.
- My ignorance of how God fashioned my brain has kept me in many ways "at the entrance to the Christian life."
- I've often blamed my emotional reactions, leadership mistakes, and intrusive thoughts "on the devil."

As I continue my journey into learning how the brain works, it is making me a better leader. As I learn more about how the brain impacts, for example, personal productivity, emotional control, healthy teams, and change management, I'm putting new tools into my leadership toolbox. I trust reading this book has done the same for you.

Perhaps the greatest benefit I've experienced is a deeper awe of the God I serve. By gaining a deeper appreciation of this amazing three-pound God-created thing called the brain, I more deeply identify with what Psalm 139:1-14 says, especially verse 14:

> LORD, you have examined me.
>> You know me.
> You know when I sit down and when I stand up.
>> Even from far away, you comprehend my plans.
> You study my traveling and resting.
>> You are thoroughly familiar with all my ways.
> There isn't a word on my tongue, LORD,
>> that you don't already know completely.
> You surround me—front and back.
>> You put your hand on me.
> That kind of knowledge is too much for me;
>> it's so high above me that I can't fathom it.
>
> Where could I go to get away from your spirit?
>> Where could I go to escape your presence?

If I went up to heaven, you would be there.

    If I went down to the grave, you would be there too!

If I could fly on the wings of dawn,

        stopping to rest only on the far side of the ocean—

            even there your hand would guide me;

            even there your strong hand would hold me tight!

If I said, "The darkness will definitely hide me;

        the light will become night around me,"

even then the darkness isn't too dark for you!

        Nighttime would shine bright as day,

        because darkness is the same as light to you!

You are the one who created my innermost parts;

        you knit me together while I was still in my mother's womb.

I give thanks to you that I was marvelously set apart.

        Your works are wonderful—I know that very well. (emphasis added)

I hope that you, too, have gained a greater appreciation for the gift of the mind and the brain and that you've been motivated to steward it more wisely.

So, where do we go from here?

First, continue the learning journey about the mind and the brain. Scientists will never fully unpack the brain's mysteries, because it's so interwoven with our soul that it transcends complete understanding. Nevertheless, I believe that a thirst for learning points to a healthy leader. Learn all you can about this God-given gift called the brain.

Second, as you read about and study the brain, do so with discernment. Some research is done by materialists who give little credence to our eternal souls. Fortunately, increasing numbers of scientists believe we are more than hormonal secretions and neuronal firings. As I wrote earlier, neuroscience is like a magnifying glass that helps us see things we otherwise could not see. But a magnifying glass requires a good light source for it to work well. God's word is that light source. Keep God's word first and foremost in your minds and hearts. Let it be the sieve through which you sift what you read. As you read about the brain, glean the good even from those who hold a different worldview than you. Remember, all truth is God's truth.

Third, talk about the brain in your daily conversations with your leaders. After all, we can't live one second without it. Help your leaders, board members, volunteers, and employees understand how the brain can help them live life and do leadership in a more God-honoring way. Put this book in the hands of your leaders. Encourage them to read it.

Finally, use the leader's guide in the next chapter to help you teach these concepts to your leaders. I've suggested six training sessions centered around six subject areas I wrote about in the book. If you invest the time to train your team, I believe it will yield tangible and lasting benefits.

I pray that God will enrich your life, your relationships, and your work as you gain a greater appreciation for the gift of the brain given to us all.

The science behind... ***Brain Surprise 11:*** *Simply changing your posture could brighten your day.*

In one research study in Israel, Dr. Tal Shafir looked at the impact of movement on the brain of twenty-two young male and female participants (Nuwer, 2013). They looked at video clips of actors performing various emotions that corresponded to sad, fearful, happy, or neutral. Happy movements included raising their arms in the air, skipping, and jumping. Sad movements included closing their chests and slumping forward. The participants then either mimicked the movements or imagined themselves doing them. The emotions they reported mirrored the corresponding movements. So, if you need a mood boost, keep a good posture or throw your arms up and out into the air.

Chapter 12

Team Development Plan

Brain Surprise 12: *Exercise is one of the best behaviors that can help us overcome food, drug, smoking, or other dependencies.*

I n this chapter I've boiled down the essence of the main concepts into an easy-to-digest outline. I've included key scriptures, core metaphors, chapter references, and concept summaries for these six subject areas:

1. the brain itself

2. emotional regulation

3. personal productivity

4. team collaboration

5. change management

6. the three overlooked competencies

In order to get these concepts deeper into your team, I'd suggest scheduling six sessions with them over six to twelve weeks to review the material and discuss the questions and exercises I've included. You can visit my website at www.charlesstone.com to download helpful tools to supplement your team's learning.

Before each session, ask your team to read the corresponding chapters. You also might find it helpful to ask each team member to teach part of each lesson. When we teach something, we always learn it better.

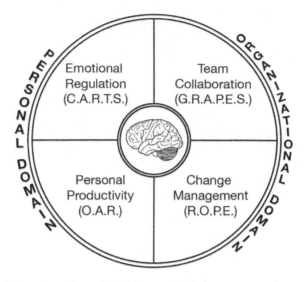

The Brain Itself (See Chapters 4 and 5)

- Key verses
  - o "I give thanks to you that I was marvelously set apart. Your works are wonderful—I know that very well." (Ps 139:14)
  - o "He replied, '*You must love the Lord your God with all your heart, with all your being,* and with all your mind." (Matt 22:37)
  - o "Don't be conformed to the patterns of this world, but be transformed by the renewing of your minds so that you can figure out what God's will is—what is good and pleasing and mature." (Rom 12:2)
  - o "Or don't you know that your body is a temple of the Holy Spirit who is in you? Don't you know that you have the Holy Spirit from God, and you don't belong to yourselves? You have been bought and paid for, so honor God with your body." (1 Cor 6:19-20)
- Key metaphors
  - o **Tootsie Pop:** represents our three brains: the lizard, mammalian, and thinking brain
    - ¬ *The lizard brain:* on autopilot and acts without thinking

¬ *The mammalian brain:* the seat of emotions, also somewhat on autopilot

¬ *The thinking brain:* serves as the brain's executive center, where thinking, analyzing, choosing, creating, symbolizing, and observing occur

o **Walnut:** like a walnut, the brain is split into two halves, with the right side operating more holistically (sees the forest) and the left side operating in a more narrow way (sees the trees). The hills and valleys (sulci and gyri) provide more real estate for the brain to operate.

o **House:** the brain is like a house. The rooms are the lobes (five) and other subcortical structures, and the building blocks are brain cells (neurons).

¬ The lobes

* *Occipital lobe:* receives and processes visual information, such as color and motion

* *Parietal lobe:* processes sensory information, such as body awareness, environmental awareness, and touch; the what and where

* *Temporal lobe:* processes hearing, language, and memory

* *Frontal lobe:* where the brain's executive center is found

* *Insular lobe:* receives sensory input from what some call our second brain, the hollow organs like our intestines and heart; also processes taste and touch

¬ *Neurons:* talk to each other (think of billions of Mousetrap games) in an "electrical to chemical to electrical to chemical process" mediated by brain chemicals called neurotransmitters

¬ *Neuroplasticity:* happens when neurons reconfigure and rewire themselves; this process allows us to learn and remember.

¬ *Neurogenesis:* happens when new brain cells are formed

185

- Key concepts
  - o *Organizing principle:* minimize danger—maximize reward that results in an away or a toward state.
  - o *Operational process:* the *X-system,* from the "x" in the word *reflexive* and the *C-system,* from the "c" in the word *reflective* (Lieberman, 2006). The X-system engages the parts of the brain that act spontaneously and impulsively, primarily our lizard and mammalian brains (the low road, which is fast). The C-system engages parts of the brain that act with intention, regulate emotions, and think before acting, our thinking center (the high road, which is slower).
- Eight key players
  - o *CEO* (prefrontal cortex): the brain's director and delegator. Executive functions operate from here.
  - o *Panic Alarm* (limbic system, where the amygdalae lie): flight-fight-freeze-appease functions operate here.
  - o *Impulse Brake* (ventral lateral prefrontal cortex): as part of the *CEO* it helps us control impulses and calm emotions.
  - o *Error Detector* (anterior cingulate cortex): detects error and monitors conflict, alerting the brain when it senses something isn't right.
  - o *Accountant* (orbitofrontal cortex, also called the medial prefrontal cortex): acts like an accountant or analyst that keeps track of memories by calculating the pros and cons of a pending decision to provide a mental balance sheet of the risks and rewards for the action center of the brain (Pilay, 2011, Kindle e-book loc. 677); also tracks the emotional value of experiences, what we like and don't like, and our preferences and values (Wolpert, 2010).
  - o *Automatic Transmission* (basal ganglia): stores habits.
  - o *Rememberer* (hippocampus and temporal lobes): converts short-term memory into long-term memory in the rest of the brain, a process called consolidation.
  - o *Rewarder-Motivator* (ventral striatum, which includes the nucleus accumbens): rewards and motivates us through the

use of neurotransmitters, especially dopamine; very important for learning.

Training Suggestions/Application

- Review the fundamental parts of the brain, and pay particular
  attention to the organizing principle, the operational process,
  the *CEO*, and the *Panic Alarm*. Be sure to use the metaphors and
  visual images to maximize memory retention.

- Discuss answers to these questions:
  - o How can understanding the brain's fundamentals help your
    team lead more effectively?
  - o What specific work environment changes could you or your
    team make to help keep the *CEO* in charge and avoid engag-
    ing the *Panic Alarm*?

Core Competencies in the Personal Domain

Emotional Regulation: CARTS *(See Chapter 6)*

- Key verses
  - o "But the fruit of the Spirit is love, joy, peace, patience, kind-
    ness, goodness, faithfulness, gentleness, and self-control.
    There is no law against things like this." (Gal 5:22-23)

- **Key concept:** The brain's *Panic Alarm* can often hijack the *CEO*'s
  thinking. It's like an inner spiritual tug-of-war the Apostle Paul
  writes about in Romans 7:15, "I don't know what I'm doing,
  because I don't do what I want to do. Instead, I do the thing that
  I hate." The CARTS acronym provides specific steps for cooperating with the Holy Spirit to keep the *CEO* in the driver's seat.

- The anatomy of an emotion
  - o stimulus (threat or reward in some internal or external
    context) >>
  - o emotion (at an unconscious level, starts within one-fifth of a
    second) >>

 o feeling (we become conscious of the emotion within half of a second) >>

 o thinking (attention, assessment, interpretation, decision) >>

 o response (an action in response to both the feeling and our assessment of the situation)

- Emotional regulation through CARTS
 o *Change your circumstances.*
  ¬ *Key concept:* situation selection
 o *Alter your attention.*
  ¬ *Key concept:* distraction
 o *Reframe the situation.*
  ¬ *Key concept:* reappraisal
  ¬ *Important tool:* a coach
 o *Tag your emotions.*
  ¬ *Key concept:* labeling
  ¬ *Important tool:* journaling
 o *Step back.*
  ¬ *Key concept:* self-distancing
  ¬ *Important tool:* an image of a camera viewfinder

Training Suggestions/Application

- In a training session, think of a real or imagined scenario in your context that would be conducive for the *Panic Alarm* to take over. Discuss how you could use each aspect of CARTS to keep your emotions from inhibiting your *CEO.*

- Role-play imaginary heated conversations between two people and have the one whose *Panic Alarm* is most likely to activate "think out loud" in real time how he or she is using various parts of CARTS to calm the *Panic Alarm.*

- As the leader, consider the merits of investing resources in providing coaching for your team.

Personal Productivity: OAR (See Chapter 7)

- Key verses
  - o "So be careful to live your life wisely, not foolishly. Take advantage of every opportunity because these are evil times." (Eph 5:15-16)
  - o "Let me know my end, Lord. How many days do I have left? I want to know how brief my time is." (Ps 39:4)
- Improving personal productivity through OAR
  - o *Optimization:* relates to mental load and brain space
    - ¬ Put first things first: prioritize prioritizing
    - ¬ Exercise
    - ¬ Sleep
    - ¬ Simplify the complex
    - ¬ Group similar information through chunking
  - o *Attention:* relates to focus and inhibiting distractions
    - ¬ Considerations:
      - * The inverted "U" and neurotransmitters
      - * Synchrony
      - * Attentional networks
    - ¬ Steps to improving attention:
      - * Increase interest
      - * Take brain breaks
      - * Avoid multitasking
  - o *Reflection:* relates to mindful awareness
    - ¬ *Four mindfulness concepts:*
      - * *Intention:* intending to pay attention to the present
      - * *Presence:* attending to what is at the moment
      - * *Nonjudgmental:* noticing an emotion rather than ascribing value to it
      - * *Beginner's mind:* approaching our thoughts and emotions as a child

189

¬ *The BEETS mindfulness plan:*

* *Body* awareness

* *Environment* awareness

* *Emotions* awareness

* *Thoughts* awareness

* *Soul* awareness

Training Suggestions/Application

- Have team members rate themselves on a scale of 0 to 5, with 0 being "nonexistent" and 5 being "very strong," on how well they are applying each of the optimization suggestions. Have them share their strongest and weakest areas and how they might improve.

- Discuss the three steps to improving attention and ways team members can remind each other to keep these areas in mind each day.

- Discuss the BEETS process and then ask your team members to find a quiet place to practice BEETS. Reconvene in thirty minutes to discuss the experience.

- Challenge your team members to try BEETS each day for seven days then report back on their experience in a week.

Core Competencies in the Organizational Domain

Team Collaboration: GRAPES (See Chapter 8)

- Building high-performing teams through GRAPES
  - o *Golden rule your team:* fairness (Matt 7:12)
    - ¬ Authentically model and communicate fairness.
    - ¬ Build trust.

¬ Recognize those who go above and beyond the call of duty.

¬ Gauge how fair others perceive you are.

o *Reduce ambiguity:* certainty (Heb 11:1)

¬ Be clear about roles and expectations.

¬ Overcommunicate.

¬ Turn ambiguities into probabilities.

¬ Set goals.

¬ Recognize that some people need more certainty.

¬ Be consistent in how you show up each day at work.

o *Allow freedom:* autonomy (Josh 25:15)

¬ Give team members choices in how they do their job.

¬ Guard against micromanaging.

¬ Monitor the team's stress level.

¬ Find what intrinsically motivates each team member, and give him or her assignments in those areas.

o *Promote personal value:* status (many scriptures elevate the status of others; Matt 25:45 is one example, "Then he will answer, 'I assure you that when you haven't done it for one of the least of these, you haven't done it for me.'")

¬ Tell your team members that you value them.

¬ Help them make progress in their work.

¬ Teach what healthy comparison looks like.

¬ Develop thorough orientation processes.

¬ Value your team's input and insight.

o *Encourage community:* relatedness (Acts 2.42)

¬ Provide regular relationship-building opportunities.

¬ Create physical gathering places that encourage socialization.

¬ Encourage your team to step into the shoes of one another to see one another's perspective.

¬ Encourage teams to create shared goals.

¬ Build an attitude of gratitude.

¬ Use humor.

o ***Smile a lot:*** mirror neurons (Prov 16:15)
  ¬ Learn to genuinely empathize with other people's pain.
  ¬ Pay attention to your team's facial expressions and body language.
  ¬ Stay aware of your own demeanor.
  ¬ Maximize face-to-face communications with your team.
  ¬ Don't mirror back anger.
  ¬ Relax.

Training Suggestions/Application

- On a scale of 0 to 5, with 0 being "nonexistent" and 5 being "very strong," have your team rate the relative strength of each domain of GRAPES in your organization. Discuss what qualities prompted the team to rank the highest domain of GRAPES as they did. Do the same for the weakest area. What needs to change to improve the lowest domain?
- Ask each team member to share what he or she perceives in you are the top two behaviors of the thirty-one listed earlier where you show the greatest strength and consistency, and why.
- Ask each team member to suggest one area in the list of thirty-one in your leadership that if improved could make you a better leader.

Change Management: ROPE *(See Chapter 9)*

- Making your change stick through ROPE
  o ***Recognize why the brain resists change.***
    ¬ The tug-of-war between the familiar and easy and the unfamiliar and hard (the needed change)
    ¬ Cognitive dissonance
    ¬ Changing resistance over time
    ¬ Social threats
  o ***Organize your thoughts around a brain-friendly buy-in plan.***
    ¬ Step into their shoes.
    ¬ Envision the benefits.

¬ Manage expectations.

¬ Invite input.

¬ Seed your culture with a change mentality.

o *Persuade with brain-friendly messaging.*

¬ Help your team see progress.

¬ Help your team act "as if."

¬ Frame your change with the audience in mind (avoidance or approach mind-set, motivation or instruction needed).

¬ Personally connect to your audience.

¬ Repeat the common why and delegate the how.

o *Evaluate through brain-friendly feedback.*

¬ Keep people informed about progress, and welcome their input.

¬ Continue to acknowledge that change is scary.

¬ Tell stories of those who successfully navigate change.

¬ Stay connected to your biggest resisters.

Training Suggestions/Application

• Think about a change you are currently trying to accomplish or one that you are contemplating. How well have you incorporated each of the ROPE domains?

• In a team meeting write out each domain of ROPE on a whiteboard and leave space beneath each one. Brainstorm specific tasks you can incorporate into your change plan related to each domain. Reduce each list to no more than four activities per domain. Create an action plan that implements these tasks into the change initiative.

Three Brain-Friendly Skills Easily Overlooked

• The three skills

o Brainstorming and creativity

¬ Encourage debate using healthy debate rules.

¬ Incorporate diversity.

¬ Appoint an affirming leader who gives everyone equal footing.

¬ Don't allow anyone to dominate.

¬ Watch for social loafing.

¬ Encourage counterintuitive solutions.

¬ Give an incubation period to allow ideas to simmer.

o Giving answers vs. fostering insight

¬ Daydreaming: encourage it

¬ Mood: use humor

¬ Location: encourage discovery of where insight best occurs for team members

¬ Application: immediately apply insight or record it to act upon later

¬ Speed: don't rush

¬ Pattern: permission, placement, questions, clarifying

o Feedback and performance reviews (the "C"s)

¬ Community: reviewer and reviewee have a relational connection

¬ Coachability: help reviewee see value of feedback

¬ Connected to goals: connect feedback to reviewee's goals

¬ Content vs. person focused: focus on tasks and not personality defects

¬ Credible: remain unbiased and knowledgeable

¬ Clarify through self-feedback: use an instrument that asks reviewee to evaluate himself or herself first

¬ Coaching: follow up to ensure and reinforce progress

¬ Closeness: give feedback as soon as you can after you become aware of the behavior that needs changing

¬ Collaborative: include peers and supervisors

¬ Culture infused: build a feedback mind-set into your culture so it won't seem so foreign and scary when it comes

Training Suggestions/Application

- You may want to schedule individual sessions for each of these three skills.
  - o Before your next brainstorming session, teach the above practices and then use them when brainstorming.
  - o Begin to personally apply the tips on fostering insight when your team members come to you with problems. Design a training session on insight by role-playing the difference between giving answers and fostering insight.
  - o Periodically teach your team about feedback so that it won't elicit as much of an away response when it's given.

It's one thing to simply read a book and hope we remember and apply its content. It's another thing to truly implement its concepts. I encourage you as a leader to take your team through the book to read and process it together. Wrestle with these concepts. Debate their merits. Apply what will work for you in your leadership. And keep brain-friendly thinking before your teams in such a consistent way that your teams truly benefit from them.

I leave you with this verse that reinforces the incredible importance our minds play in life and leadership.

*"You must love the Lord your God with all your heart, with all your being, with all your strength, **and with all your mind**, and love your neighbor as yourself."* (Luke 10:27, emphasis added)

The science behind...*Brain Surprise 12:* Exercise is one of the best behaviors that can help us overcome food, drug, smoking, or other dependencies.

Dr. John Ratey, author of *Spark: The Revolutionary New Science of Exercise and the Brain*, has extensively studied the effects of exercise on the brain and its effects on dependencies like food and drugs. Dependencies fuel our brain's hunger for dopamine in our *Rewarder-Motivator*, the nucleus accumbens, and often gets the *Panic Alarm* involved when it senses a dopamine deficit. Exercise provides a healthy way to gradually increase dopamine levels to give us that sense of well-being that dependencies temporarily give us, only with a dependency it's often destructive. Exercise also calms our *Panic Alarm*. It creates new connections that provide alternative choices than can help us bypass the brain's addictive pathways.

Reference List

Ally, B. A., & Budson, A. E. (2007, March). The worth of pictures: Using high density event-related potentials to understand the memorial power of pictures and the dynamics of recognition memory. *NeuroImage, 35*(1), 378–95.

Amabile, T. M., Kramer, S. J., Bonabeau, E., Bingham, A., Litan, R. E., Klein, J., & Ross, C. (2010, January). The HBR list: Breakthrough ideas for 2010. *Harvard Business Review.* Retrieved from https://hbr.org/2010/01/the-hbr -list-breakthrough-ideas-for-2010/ar/1

Ambady, N., LaPlante, D., Nguyen, T., Rosenthal, R., Chaumeton, N., & Levinson, W. (2002, July). Surgeons' tone of voice: A clue to malpractice history. *Surgery, 132*(1), 5–9.

Anderson, C., Kraus, M. W., Galinsky, A. D., & Keltner, D. (2012, July 1). The local-ladder effect: Social status and subjective well-being. *Psychological Science, 23*(7), 764–71.

Armour, J. A. (2004, August 1). Cardiac neuronal hierarchy in health and disease. *American Journal of Physiology—Regulatory, Integrative and Comparative Physiology, 287*(2), R262–R271.

Ashford, S. J., Blatt, R., & VadeWalle, D. (2003). Reflections on the looking glass: A review of research on feedback-seeking behavior in organizations. *Journal of Management, 29*(6), 773–99.

Atwater, L. E., & Brett, J. F. (2005). Antecedents and consequences of reactions to developmental 360° feedback. *Journal of Vocational Behavior, 66*(3), 532–48.

Baikie, K. A., & Wilhelm, K. (2005). Emotional and physical health benefits of expressive writing. *Advances in Psychiatric Treatment, 11*(5), 338–46.

Baron, S., & Schmidt, R. A. (1991). Operational aspects of retail franchises. *International Journal of Retail & Distribution Management, 19*(2). Available from http://www.emeraldinsight.com/doi/abs/10.1108/09590559110135061

Barsade, S. G. (2002, December). The ripple effect: Emotional contagion and its influence on group behavior. *Administrative Science Quarterly, 47*(4), 644–75.

Batista, E. (2009, November 18). David Rock on neuroscience, coaching and leadership. Retrieved from http://www.edbatista.com/2009/11/david-rock.html

Baumeister, R. F., Bratslavsky, E., Finkenauer, C., & Vohs, K. D. (2001). Bad is stronger than good. *Review of General Psychology, 5*(4), 323–70.

Baumgartner, T., Heinrichs, M., Vonlanthen, A., Fischbacher, U., & Fehr, E. (2008, May 22). Oxytocin shapes the neural circuitry of trust and trust adaptation in humans. *Neuron, 58*(4), 639–50.

Beeman, M. (n.d.). *Insight in the brain.* Retrieved from http://groups.psych.northwestern.edu/mbeeman/PLoS_Supp.htm

Beeney, J. E., Franklin, R. G., Jr., Levy, K. N., & Adams, R. B., Jr. (2011). I feel your pain: Emotional closeness modulates neural responses to empathically experienced rejection. *Social Neuroscience, 6*(4), 369–76.

Bennett, D. (2012, October 17). What does the marshmallow test actually test? *Bloomberg BusinessWeek.* Retrieved from http://www.businessweek.com/articles/2012-10-17/what-does-the-marshmallow-test-actually-test

Berkman, E. T. (2012, November 12). *Goals, motivation, and the brain.* Retrieved from http://www.psychologytoday.com/blog/the-motivated-brain/201211/goals-motivation-and-the-brain

Betz, A. (2011, December 1). Balance coaching, also known as reframing, reappraisal and perspectives [Blog]. Retrieved from http://yourcoachingbrain.wordpress.com/2011/12/01/balance-coaching-also-known-as-reframing-reappraisal-and-perspectives/

Bippus, A. M. (2000, January). Making sense of humor in young romantic relationships: Understanding partners' perceptions. *Humor - International Journal of Humor Research, 13*(4), 395–418.

Bishop, S. J. (2007, July). Neurocognitive mechanisms of anxiety: An integrative account. *Trends in Cognitive Sciences, 11*(7), 307–16.

Bregman, P. (2010, May 20). How (and why) to stop multitasking. *Harvard Business Review*. Retrieved from https://hbr.org/2010/05/how-and-why-to-stop-multitaski.html

Brennan, A. R., & Arnsten, A. F. T. (2008, May). Neuronal mechanisms underlying attention deficit hyperactivity disorder. *Annals of the New York Academy of Sciences, 1129*, 236–45.

Brown, K. W., & Ryan, R. M. (2003, April). The benefits of being present: Mindfulness and its role in psychological well-being. *Journal of Personality and Social Psychology, 84*(4), 822–48.

Burklund, L. J., Eisenberger, N. I., & Lieberman, M. D. (2007, January). The face of rejection: Rejection sensitivity moderates dorsal anterior cingulate activity to disapproving facial expressions. *Social Neuroscience, 2*(3-4), 238–53.

Cacioppo, J. T., & Patrick, W. (2009). *Loneliness: Human nature and the need for social connection* (reprint ed.). New York, NY: W. W. Norton.

Castro, J. (2010, November 24). A wandering mind is an unhappy one. *Scientific American*. Retrieved from http://www.scientificamerican.com/article/a-wandering-mind-is-an-un/

CDC. (2013). *Insufficient sleep is a public health epidemic*. Retrieved from http://www.cdc.gov/features/dssleep/

Chalquist, C. (n.d.). *In the words of Alfred Adler*. Retrieved from http://www.terrapsych.com/adler.html

Chambers, O. (1992). *My utmost for his highest: An updated edition in today's language*. Grand Rapids, MI: Discovery House Publishers.

Chen, Z., Williams, K. D., Fitness, J., & Newton, N. C. (2008, August). When hurt will not heal: Exploring the capacity to relieve social and physical pain. *Psychological Science, 19*(8), 789–95.

Christoff, K., Gordon, A. M., Smallwood, J., Smith, R., & Schooler, J. W. (2009, May 26). Experience sampling during fMRI reveals default network and executive system contributions to mind wandering. *Proceedings of the National Academy of Sciences, 106*(21), 8719–24.

Cicero, L., Pierro, A., & Van Knippenberg, D. (2010, June). Leadership and uncertainty: How role ambiguity affects the relationship between leader group prototypicality and leadership effectiveness. *British Journal of Management, 21*(2), 411–21.

Clarke, A. (1824). *Memoirs of the Wesley family.* New York: N. Bangs and T. Mason, for The Methodist Episcopal Church. Retrieved from http://archive.org /details/memoirswesleyfa00clargoog

Cohen, J. R., Berkman, E. T., & Lieberman, M. D. (2013). Intentional and incidental self-control in ventrolateral PFC. In D. T. Stuss & R. T. Knight (Eds.), *Principles of frontal lobe function* (2nd ed.) (pp. 417–40). New York: NY: Oxford University Press.

Colcombe, S. J., Erickson, K. I., Scalf, P. E., Kim, J. S., Prakash, R., McAuley, E., Elavksy, S., Marquez, D. X., Hu, L., & Kramer, A. F. (2006). *The Journals of Gerontology: Series A: Biological Sciences and Medical Sciences, 61*(11), 1166– 70.

Cope, M. (2003). *The seven Cs of consulting: The definitive guide to the consulting process* (2nd ed.). Upper Saddle River, NJ: FT Press.

Cross, E. S., Hamilton, A. F. de C., Kraemer, D. J. M., Kelley, W. M., & Grafton, S. T. (2009). Dissociable substrates for body motion and physical experience in the human action observation network. *European Journal of Neuroscience, 30*, 1383–92.

CubeSmart. (2002). *Social interruption and the loss of productivity.* Retrieved from http://interruptions.net/literature/CubeSmart-productivity-wp1.pdf

De Boer, E., Bakker, A. B., Syroid, J. E., & Schaufeli, W. (2002). Unfairness at work as a predictor of absenteeism. *Journal of Organizational Behavior, 23*, 181–97.

Decety, J. (2010, July). To what extent is the experience of empathy mediated by shared neural circuits? *Emotion Review, 2*(3), 204–7.

De Dreu, C. K. W. (2012, March). Oxytocin modulates cooperation within and competition between groups: An integrative review and research agenda. *Hormones and Behavior, 61*(3), 419–28.

de Groot, A. D. (1965). *Thought and choice in chess.* The Hague, The Netherlands: Mouton.

Delgado, M. R., Frank, R. H., & Phelps, E. A. (2005). Perceptions of moral character modulate the neural systems of reward during the trust game. *Nature Neuroscience, 8*(11), 1611–18.

DeNisi, A., & Kluger, A. N. (2000). Feedback effectiveness: Can 360-degree appraisals be improved? *The Academy of Management Executive, 14*(1), 129–39.

DePaulo, B. M., Kashy, D. A., Kirkendol, S. E., Wyer, M. M., & Epstein, J. A. (1996, May). Lying in everyday life. *Journal of Personality and Social Psychology, 70*(5), 979–95.

Desmurget, M., & Sirigu, A. (2009, October). A parietal-premotor network for movement intention and motor awareness. *Trends in Cognitive Sciences, 13*(10), 411–19.

Dewall, C. N., Macdonald, G., Webster, G. D., Masten, C. L., Baumeister, R. F., Powell, C., Combs, D., Schurtz, D. R., Stillman, T. F., Tice, D. M., & Eisenberger, N. I. (2010, July). Acetaminophen reduces social pain: Behavioral and neural evidence. *Psychological Science, 21*(7), 931–37.

Dhont, K., Roets, A., & Hiel, A. V. (2011, April). Opening closed minds: The combined effects of intergroup contact and need for closure on prejudice. *Personality and Social Psychology Bulletin, 37*(4), 514–28.

Dijksterhuis, A., & Nordgren, L. F. (2006, June). A theory of unconscious thought. *Perspectives on Psychological Science, 1*(2), 95–109.

Dimoka, A., Adomavicius, G., Gupta, A., & Pavlou, P. A. (Forthcoming). *Reducing the cognitive overload in continuous combinatorial auctions: Evidence from an fMRI study.* Retrieved from http://www.fox.temple.edu/minisites/neural/publications.html

Dinges, D. F., Pack, F., Williams, K., Gillen, K. A., Powerll, J. W., Ott, G. E., Aptowicz, C., & Pack, A. I. (1997). Cumulative sleepiness, mood disturbance and psychomotor vigilance performance decrements during a week of sleep restricted to 4–5 hours per night. *Sleep: Journal of Sleep Research & Sleep Medicine, 20*(4), 267–77.

Dixon, P., Rock, D., & Ochsner, K. N. (2010). Turn the 360 around. *Neuroleadership Journal, 3*, 1–9.

Dobbs, D. (2006, September 12). A must-see: Mirror neurons in yo' face [Blog]. Retrieved from http://scienceblogs.com/neuronculture/2006/09/12/a-mustsee-mirror-neurons-in-yo/

Duhigg, C. (2012). The golden rule of habit change. *Psych Central.* Retrieved from http://psychcentral.com/blog/archives/2012/07/17/the-golden-rule-of -habit-change/

Duhigg, C. (2012, June 7). Habits: Why we do what we do. *Harvard Business Re-view.* Retrieved from https://hbr.org/2012/06/habits-why-we-do-what -we-do

Eisenberger, N. I. (2012, February). The neural bases of social pain: Evidence for shared representations with physical pain. *Psychosomatic Medicine, 74*(2), 126–35.

Eisenberger, N. I., Inagaki, T. K., Muscatell, K. A., Byrne Haltom, K. E., & Leary, M. R. (2011, November). The neural sociometer: Brain mechanisms under-lying state self-esteem. *Journal of Cognitive Neuroscience, 23*(11), 3448–55.

Ellenberg, J. (2012, March 23). Six degrees of innovation. *Slate.* Retrieved from http://www.slate.com/articles/life/do_the_math/2012/03/how_creativity _works_what_broadway_musicals_really_teach_us_about_collaboration _.html

Elwart, S. (2013). *Information overload making your head explode?.* Retrieved from http://www.wnd.com/2013/01/information-overload-making-your-head -explode/

Epel, E., Daubenmier, J., Moskowitz, J. T., Folkman, S., & Blackburn, E. (2009). Can meditation slow rate of cellular aging? Cognitive stress, mindfulness, and telomeres. *Annals of the New York Academy of Sciences, 1172*, 34–53.

Falk, E. B., Berkman, E. T., Mann, T., Harrison, B., & Lieberman, M. D. (2010, June 23). Predicting persuasion-induced behavior change from the brain. *The Journal of Neuroscience, 30*(25), 8421–24.

Falk, E. B., O'Donnell, M. B., & Lieberman, M. D. (2012). Getting the word out: Neural correlates of enthusiastic message propagation. *Frontiers in Human Neuroscience, 6*(313).

Famous scientists who believed in God. (2011, December 8). Retrieved from http:// www.godandscience.org/apologetics/sciencefaith.html

Foerde, K., Knowlton, B. J., & Poldrack, R. A. (2006, August 1). Modulation of competing memory systems by distraction. *Proceedings of the National Acad-emy of Sciences, 103*(31), 11778–83.

Ford, M. B., & Collins, N. L. (2010, March). Self-esteem moderates neuro-endocrine and psychological responses to interpersonal rejection. *Journal of Personality and Social Psychology, 98*(3), 405–19.

Förster, J., Friedman, R. S., & Liberman, N. (2004, August). Temporal construal effects on abstract and concrete thinking: Consequences for insight and creative cognition. *Journal of Personality and Social Psychology, 87*(2), 177–89.

Fournier, J. C., DeRubeis, R. J., Hollon, S. D., Dimidjian, S., Amsterdam, J. D., Shelton, R. C., & Fawcett, J. (2010, January 6). Antidepressant drug effects and depression severity: A patient-level meta-analysis. *JAMA: The Journal of the American Medical Association, 303*(1), 47–53.

Gallese, V., Fadiga, L., Fogassi, L., & Rizzolatti, G. (1996, April). Action recognition in the premotor cortex. *Brain, 119*(2), 593–609.

Georgia Health Sciences University. (2011, February 28). Brain's 'reward' center also responds to bad experiences. *ScienceDaily*. Retrieved from www.sciencedaily.com/releases/2011/02/110222121913.htm

Giang, V. (2012, October 24). Workers would rather have a better boss than a salary increase. *Business Insider*. Retrieved from http://www.businessinsider.com/workers-want-better-bosses-gallup-michelle-mcquaid-2012-10

Gijsbers, A. J. (2003, July). *The dialogue between neuroscience and theology*. Retrieved from http://www.iscast.org/rough_diamonds/past_papers/Gijsbers_A_2003-07_Neuroscience_and_Theology.pdf

Gilbert, A. (2005, March 28). Why can't you pay attention anymore? *CNET*. Retrieved from http://news.cnet.com/Why-cant-you-pay-attention-anymore/2100-1022_3-5637632.html

Glasser, J. (2013, February 28). Your brain is hooked on being right. *Harvard Business Review*. Retrieved from https://hbr.org/2013/02/break-your-addiction-to-being/

Godwin, D., & Cham, J. (2012, October 18). Your brain by the numbers. *Scientific American Mind, 23*(5). Retrieved and adapted from http://www.scientificamerican.com/article/mind-in-pictures-your-brain-by-the-numbers/

Goh, J. O., & Park, D. C. (2009). Neuroplasticity and cognitive aging: The scaffolding theory of aging and cognition. *Restorative Neurology and Neuroscience, 27*(5), 391–403.

Goldin, P. R., McRae, K., Ramel, W., & Gross, J. J. (2008, March 15). The neural bases of emotion regulation: Reappraisal and suppression of negative emotion. *Biological Psychiatry, 63*(6), 577–86.

Goleman, D., & Boyatzis, R. (2008, September). Social intelligence and the biology of leadership. *Harvard Business Review.* Retrieved from http://hbr .org/2008/09/social-intelligence-and-the-biology-of-leadership/ar/1

Gordon, E. (2000). *Integrative neuroscience: Bringing together biological, psychological, and clinical models of the human brain.* Singapore: Harwood Academic Publishers.

Gordon, E., Barnett, K. J., Cooper, N. J., Tran, N., & Williams, L. M. (2008, September). An "integrative neuroscience" platform: Application to profiles of negativity and positivity bias. *Journal of Integrative Neuroscience, 7*(3), 354–66.

Gottman, J., Gonso, J., & Rasmussen, B. (1975, September). Social interaction, social competence, and friendship in children. *Child Development, 46*(3), 709–18.

Green, J. B. (2008). *Body, soul and human life.* Grand Rapids, MI: Baker Academic.

Green, J. D., Nystrom, L. E., Engell, A. D., Darley, J. M., & Cohen, J. D. (2004, October 14). The neural bases of cognitive conflict and control in moral judgment. *Neuron, 44*(2), 389–400.

Gross, J. J. (2002, May). Emotion regulation: Affective, cognitive, and social consequences. *Psychophysiology, 39*(3), 281–91.

Gross, J. J., & John, O. P. (2003, August). Individual differences in two emotion regulation processes: Implications for affect, relationships, and well-being. *Journal of Personality and Social Psychology, 85*(2), 348–62.

Hadhazy, A. (2010, February 12). Think twice: How the gut's "second brain" influences mood and well-being. *Scientific American.* Retrieved from http://www .scientificamerican.com/article/gut-second-brain/

Hanson, R. (2010, October 26). *Confronting the negativity bias.* Retrieved from http://www.psychologytoday.com/blog/your-wise-brain/201010/confront ing-the-negativity-bias

Havas, D. A., Glenberg, A. M., Gutowski, K. A., Lucarelli, M. J., & Davidson,

R. J. (2010, July). Cosmetic use of botulinum toxin-a affects processing of emotional language. *Psychological Science, 21*(7), 895–900.

Hedden, T., & Gabrieli, J. D. E. (2006). The ebb and flow of attention in the human brain. *Nature Neuroscience, 9*(7), 863–65.

Hemp, P. (2009, September). Death by information overload. *Harvard Business Review.* Retrieved from https://hbr.org/2009/09/death-by-information-overload/ar/1

Herry, C., Bach, D. R., Esposito, R., Di Salle, F., Perrig, W. J., Scheffler, K., Lüthi, A., & Seifritz, E. (2007, May 30). Processing of temporal unpredictability in human and animal amygdala. *The Journal of Neuroscience, 27*(22), 5958–66.

Hickok, G. (2009). Eight problems for the mirror neuron theory of action understanding in monkeys and humans. *Journal of Cognitive Neuroscience, 21*(7), 1229–43.

Hirano, Y., Obata, T., Takahashi, H., Tachibana, A., Kuroiwa, D., Takahasti, T., Ikehira, H., & Onozuka, M. (2013, April). Effects of chewing on cognitive processing speed. *Brain and Cognition, 81*(3), 376–81.

Hölzel, B. K., Carmody, J., Vangel, M., Congleton, C., Yerramsetti, S. M., Gard, T., & Lazar, S. W. (2011, January 30). Mindfulness practice leads to increases in regional brain gray matter density. *Psychiatry Research: Neuroimaging, 191*(1), 36–43.

Hsu, M., Bhatt, M., Adolphs, R., Tranel, D., & Camerer, C. F. (2005, December 9). Neural systems responding to degrees of uncertainty in human decision-making. *Science, 310*(5754), 1680–83.

Iacoboni, M. (2009, January). Imitation, empathy, and mirror neurons. *Annual Review of Psychology, 60*(1), 653–70.

Ibarra, H. (1999, December). Provisional selves: Experimenting with image and identity in professional adaptation. *Administrative Science Quarterly, 44*(4), 764–91.

Inzlicht, M., Schmeichel, B. J., & Macrae, C. N. (2014). Why self-control seems (but may not be) limited. *Trends in Cognitive Sciences, 18*(3), 127–33.

Izuma, K., Saito, D. N., & Sadato, N. (2008, April 24). Processing of social and monetary rewards in the human striatum. *Neuron, 58*(2), 284–94.

Jabr, F. (2012, June 13). Know your neurons: What is the ratio of glia to neurons in the brain? [Blog]. Retrieved from http://blogs.scientificamerican.com /brainwaves/2012/06/13/know-your-neurons-what-is-the-ratio-of-glia-to -neurons-in-the-brain/

Johnson, S. (2003, March 1). Fear in the brain. *Discovery Magazine.* Retrieved from http://discovermagazine.com/2003/mar/cover#.UTj6w6X06EM

Jung-Beeman, M., Collier, A., & Kounios, J. (2008). How insight happens: Learning from the brain. *Neuroleadership Journal, 1,* 20–25.

Kane, M. J., & Engle, R. W. (2003, March). Working-memory capacity and the control of attention: The contributions of goal neglect, response competition, and task set to Stroop interference. *Journal of Experimental Psychology. General, 132*(1), 47–70.

Kang, S. K., Hirsh, J. B., & Chasteen, A. L. (2010). Your mistakes are mine: Self-other overlap predicts neural response to observed errors. *Journal of Experimental Social Psychology, 46*(1), 229–32.

Karau, S. J., & Hart, J. W. (1998, August). Group cohesiveness and social loafing: Effects of a social interaction manipulation on individual motivation within groups. *Group Dynamics: Theory, Research, and Practice, 2*(3), 185–91.

Kluger, A. N., & DeNisi, A. (1996). The effects of feedback interventions on performance: A historical review, a meta-analysis, and a preliminary feedback intervention theory. *Psychological Bulletin, 119*(2), 254–84. Retrieved from http://mario.gsia.cmu.edu/micro_2007/readings/feedback_effects_meta _analysis.pdf

Knäuper, B., Roseman, M., Johnson, P. J., & Krantz, L. H. (2009). Using mental imagery to enhance the effectiveness of implementation intentions. *Current Psychology, 28*(3), 181–86.

Ko, V. (2013, April 15). Can you cope with criticism at work? *CNN.* Retrieved from http://edition.cnn.com/2013/04/14/business/criticism-praise-feedback -work-life/

Koen, M., Bitzer, E. M., & Beets, P. A. D. (2012). Feedback or feed-forward? A case study in one higher education classroom. *Journal of Social Science, 3*(2), 231–42.

Koob, A. (2009, October 27). The root of thought: What do glial cells do? *Scientific*

American. Retrieved from http://www.scientificamerican.com/article/the-root-of-thought-what/

Korb, A. (2012, November 20). The grateful brain: The neuroscience of giving thanks [Blog]. Retrieved from http://www.psychologytoday.com/blog/prefrontal-nudity/201211/the-grateful-brain

Kounios, J., Frymiare, J. L., Bowden, E. M., Fleck, J. I., Subramaniam, K., Parrish, T. B., & Jung-Beeman, M. (2006). The prepared mind: Neural activity prior to problem presentation predicts subsequent solution by sudden insight. *Psychological Science, 17*(10), 882–90.

Kross, E., & Ayduk, O. (2008). Facilitating adaptive emotional analysis: Distinguishing distanced-analysis of depressive experiences from immersed-analysis and distraction. *Personality and Social Psychology Bulletin, 34*(7), 924–38.

Lambert, N. M., Clark, M. S., Durtschi, J., Fincham, F. D., & Graham, S. M. (2010). Benefits of expressing gratitude: Expressing gratitude to a partner changes one's view of the relationship. *Psychological Science, 21*(4), 574–80.

Lawrence, B. (2011). *The practice of the presence of God: The best rule of a holy life* [Kindle version]. Retrieved from Amazon.com

Layous, K., Chancellor, J., Lyubomirsky, S., Wang, L., & Doraiswamy, P. M. (2011, August). Delivering happiness: Translating positive psychology intervention research for treating major and minor depressive disorders. *The Journal of Alternative and Complementary Medicine, 17*(8), 675–83.

Lee, W., & Reeve, J. (2012). Self-determined, but not non-self-determined, motivation predicts activations in the anterior insular cortex: An fMRI study of personal agency. *Social Cognitive and Affective Neuroscience, 8*, 538–45.

Leotti, L. A., & Delgado, M. R. (2011). The inherent reward of choice. *Psychological Science, 22*(10), 1310–18.

Lieberman, M. D. (2006). Social cognitive neuroscience: A review of core processes. *Annual Review of Psychology, 58*, 259–89.

Lieberman, M. D., Eisenberger, N. I., Crockett, M. J., Tom, S. M., Pfeifer, J. H., & Way, B. M. (2007, May). Putting feelings into words: Affect labeling disrupts amygdala activity in response to affective stimuli. *Psychological Science, 18*(5), 421–28.

London, M., & Smither, J. W. (1995, December). Can multi-source feedback change perceptions of goal accomplishment, self-evaluations, and performance-related outcomes? Theory-based applications and directions for research. *Personnel Psychology, 48*(4), 803–39.

Lount, R. B., Jr., Zhong, C.-B., Sivanathan, N., & Murnighan, J. K. (2008). Getting off on the wrong foot: The timing of a breach and the restoration of trust. *Personality and Social Psychology Bulletin, 34*(12), 1601–12.

Löw, A., Lang, P. J., Smith, J. C., & Bradley, M. M. (2008, September). Both predator and prey: emotional arousal in threat and reward. *Psychological Science, 19*(9), 865–73.

Ludmer, R., Dudai, Y., & Rubin, N. (2011, March 10). Uncovering camouflage: Amygdala activation predicts long-term memory of induced perceptual insight. *Neuron, 69*(5), 1002–14.

Macdonald, G., & Leary, M. R. (2005, March). Why does social exclusion hurt? The relationship between social and physical pain. *Psychological Bulletin, 131*(2), 202–23.

Mackie, A. M., Coda, B. C., Hill, H. F. (1991, September). Adolescents use patient-controlled analgesia effectively for relief from prolonged oropharyngeal mucositis pain. *Pain, 46*(3), 265–69.

Magariños, A. M., McEwen, B. S., Flügge, G., & Fuchs, E. (1996, May 15). Chronic psychosocial stress causes apical dendritic atrophy of hippocampal CA3 pyramidal neurons in subordinate tree shrews. *The Journal of Neuroscience: The Official Journal of the Society for Neuroscience, 16*(10), 3534–40.

Manz, C. C. (1986, July). Self-leadership: Toward an expanded theory of self-influence processes in organizations. *Academy of Management Review, 11*(3), 585–600.

Mayberg, H. S., Silva, J. A., Brannan, S. K., Tekell, J. L., Mahurin, R. K., McGinnis, S., & Jerabek, P. A. (2002, May). The functional neuroanatomy of the placebo effect. *American Journal of Psychiatry, 159*(5), 728–37.

McGilchrist, I. (2009). *The master and his emissary* [Kindle version]. Retrieved from Amazon.com

McGonigal, K. (2012, August 1). *Smile your way out of stress?* Retrieved from http://www.psychologytoday.com/blog/the-science-willpower/201208/smile-your-way-out-stress

McRae, K., Ochsner, K. N., & Gross, J. J. (2011). The reason in passion: A social cognitive neuroscience approach to emotion regulation. In K. D. Vohs & R. F. Baumeister (Eds.), *Handbook of self-regulation* (2nd ed.) (pp. 186–203). New York, NY: Guilford Press.

Medina, J. (2009). *Brain rules: 12 principles for surviving and thriving at work, home, and school* (reprint ed.). Seattle, WA: Pear Press.

Meyer-Lindenberg, A., Domes, G., Kirsch, P., & Heinrichs, M. (2011, September). Oxytocin and vasopressin in the human brain: Social neuropeptides for translational medicine. *Nature Reviews Neuroscience, 12*(9), 524–38.

Mikkelsen, A., & Gundersen, M. (2003, May). The effect of a participatory organizational intervention on work environment, job stress, and subjective health complaints. *International Journal of Stress Management, 10*(2), 91–110.

Mischel, W., Ebbesen, E. B., & Raskoff Zeiss, A. (1972, February). Cognitive and attentional mechanisms in delay of gratification. *Journal of Personality and Social Psychology, 21*(2), 204–18.

Mobbs, D., Yu, R., Meyer, M., Passamonti, L., Seymour, B., Calder, A. J., Schweizer, S., Frith, C. D., & Dalgleish, T. (2009, May 15). A key role for similarity in vicarious reward. *Science, 324*(5929), 900.

Moore, E. A. (2010, November 17). Human brain has more switches than all computers on earth. *CNET*. Retrieved from http://www.cnet.com/news /human-brain-has-more-switches-than-all-computers-on-earth/

Morris, J. S., Öhman, A., & Dolan, R. J. (1999, February 16). A subcortical pathway to the right amygdala mediating "unseen" fear. *Proceedings of the National Academy of Sciences of the United States of America, 96*(4), 1680–85.

Munzert, J., Zentgraf, K., Stark, R., & Vaitl, D. (2008, July). Neural activation in cognitive motor processes: Comparing motor imagery and observation of gymnastic movements. *Experimental Brain Research, 188*(3), 437–44.

National Sleep Foundation. (n.d.). *How much sleep do we really need?*. Retrieved from http://www.sleepfoundation.org/article/how-sleep-works/how-much -sleep-do-we-really-need

Neal, D. T., Wood, W., & Quinn, J. M. (2006, August). Habits—A repeat performance. *Current Directions in Psychological Science, 15*(4), 198–202.

Nemeth, C. J., Personnaz, B., Personnaz, M., & Goncalo, J. A. (2004). The liberating role of conflict in group creativity: A study in two countries. *European Journal of Social Psychology, 34*(4), 365–74.

NeuroLeadership Institute (2013). *About neuroleadership.* Retrieved from http://www.neuroleadership.org/index.shtml

Newberg, A. (2010). *Principles of neurotheology* [Kindle version]. Retrieved from Amazon.com

Newberg, A., & Waldman, M. R. (2010). *How God changes your brain: Breakthrough findings from a leading neuroscientist* [Kindle version]. Retrieved from Amazon.com

Nolen-Hoeksema, S., Wisco, B. E., & Lyubomirsky, S. (2008, September). Rethinking rumination. *Perspectives on Psychological Science, 3*(5), 400–424.

Noll, M. A. (2011). *Jesus Christ and the life of the mind* [Kindle version]. Retrieved from Amazon.com

Nunes, J. C., & Dreze, X. (2006, April). Your loyalty program is betraying you. *Harvard Business Review.* Retrieved from http://hbr.org/2006/04/your-loyalty-program-is-betraying-you/ar/1

Nuwer, R. (2013, May 15). Boost your mood: Simple movements to make you happier. *HuffPost.* Retrieved from http://www.huffingtonpost.com/2013/05/15/boost-your-mood-dancing_n_3281107.html

O'Dell, J. (2011, May 27). *Social media distractions are costing businesses major money [STUDY].* Retrieved from http://mashable.com/2011/05/27/digital-distraction-survey/

Pagnoni, G., & Cekic, M. (2007, October). Age effects on gray matter volume and attentional performance in Zen meditation. *Neurobiology of Aging, 28*(10), 1623–27.

Parboteeah, K. P., Bronson, J. W., & Cullen, J. B. (2005, August). Does national culture affect willingness to justify ethically suspect behaviors? A focus on the GLOBE national culture scheme. *International Journal of Cross Cultural Management, 5*(2), 123–38.

Pascual-Leone, A., Amedi, A., Fregni, F., & Merabet, L. B. (2005). The plastic human brain cortex. *Annual Review of Neuroscience, 28*, 377–401.

Paul VI (1965, December 7). *Gaudium et spes.* Retrieved from http://www .vatican.va/archive/hist_councils/ii_vatian_council/documents/vat-ii_const _19651207_gaudium-et-spes_en.html

Pearrow, M. J. (2012). *Infobesity: Cognitive and physical impacts of information overconsumption.* Retrieved from http://distworkshop.files.wordpress.com /2012/01/dist2012_submission_8.pdf

Pilay, S. S. (2011). *Your brain and business: The neuroscience of great leaders* [Kindle Version]. Retrieved from Amazon.com

Pizzagalli, D. A., Sherwood, R. J., Henriques, J. B., & Davidson, R. J. (2005, October). Frontal brain asymmetry and reward responsiveness: A source-localization study. *Psychological Science, 16*(10), 805–13.

Platt, M. L., & Huettel, S. A. (2008, April). Risky business: The neuroeconomics of decision making under uncertainty. *Nature Neuroscience, 11*(4), 398–403.

Polkinghorne, J. (2007). The science and religion debate—An introduction. *Faraday Paper, 1.* Retrieved from https://www.faraday.st-edmunds.cam.ac.uk /resources/Faraday%20Papers/Faraday%20Paper%201%20Polkinghorne _EN.pdf

Prabhakaran, R., & Gray, J. R. (2012, April 26). The pervasive nature of unconscious social information processing in executive control. *Frontiers in Human Neuroscience, 6.*

Pychyl, T. A. (2001, June 20). Free won't: It may be all that we have (or need). Retrieved from http://www.psychologytoday.com/blog/dont-delay/201106 /free-wont-it-may-be-all-we-have-or-need

Rameson, L. T., Morelli, S. A., & Lieberman, M. D. (2012, January). The neural correlates of empathy: Experience, automaticity, and prosocial behavior. *Journal of Cognitive Neuroscience, 24*(1), 235–45.

Ratey, J. J. (2013). *Spark: The revolutionary new science of exercise and the brain.* New York, NY: Little, Brown and Company.

Richards, J. M., & Gross, J. J. (2006). Personality and emotional memory: How regulating emotion impairs memory for emotional events. *Journal of Research in Personality, 40*(5), 631–51.

Rizzolatti, G., & Sinigaglia, C. (2008). *Mirrors in the brain: How our minds share actions, emotions, and experience.* (F. Anderson, Trans.). New York, NY: Oxford University Press. (Original work published 2006)

Robbins, J. M., Ford, M. T., & Tetrick, L. E. (2012, March). Perceived unfairness and employee health: A meta-analytic integration. *The Journal of Applied Psychology, 97*(2), 235–72.

Robison, J. (2008, November 13). Workplace socializing is productive. *Gallup Business Journal.* Retrieved from http://www.gallup.com/businessjournal /111766/News-Flash-Workplace-Socializing-Productive.aspx

Rock, D. (2007). *Quiet leadership: Six steps to transforming performance at work* (reprint ed.). New York, NY: HarperBusiness.

Rock, D. (2008). SCARF: A brain-based model for collaborating with and influencing others. *Neuroleadership Journal, 1*, 44–52.

Rock, D. (2009). *Your brain at work: Strategies for overcoming distraction, regaining focus, and working smarter all day long.* New York, NY: HarperCollins.

Rock, D. (2011, November 10). Praise leads to cheating? *Harvard Business Review.* Retrieved from https://hbr.org/2011/11/praise-leads-to-cheating/

Rock, D., & Cox, C. (2012). SCARF in 2012: Updating the social neuroscience of collaborating with others. *Neuroleadership Journal, 4.*

Rock, D., & Page, L .J. (2009). *Coaching with the brain in mind: Foundations for practice.* Hoboken, NJ: Wiley.

Roemer, E., & Borkovec, T. D. (1994, August). Effects of suppressing thoughts about emotional material. *Journal of Abnormal Psychology, 103*(3), 467–74.

Rosen, J. B., & Donley, M. P. (2006). Animal studies of amygdala function in fear and uncertainty: Relevance to human research. *Biological Psychology, 73*(1), 49–60.

Ross, B. H., & Markman, A. (Eds.). (1990). *Categories in Use.* The psychology of learning and motivation (Vol. 47). San Diego, CA: Academic Press.

Ross, L., Greene, D., & House, P. (1977). The "false consensus effect": An egocentric bias in social perception and attribution processes. *Journal of Experimental Social Psychology, 13*(3), 279–301.

Rounding, K., Lee, A., Jacobson, J. A., & Ji, L.-J. (2012, June). Religion replenishes self-control. *Psychological Science, 23*(6), 635–42.

Ruder, D. B. (2011, May–June). The "water cooler" effect may improve scientific research. *Harvard Magazine.* Retrieved from http://harvardmagazine.com /2011/05/water-cooler-effect

Sala, F. (2003, September). Laughing all the way to the bank. *Harvard Business Review.* Retrieved from https://hbr.org/2003/09/laughing-all-the-way-to -the-bank/ar/1

Salomens, T. V., Johnstone, T., Backonja, M.-M., Shackman, A. J., & Davidson, R. J. (2007, June). Individual differences in the effects of perceived controllability on pain perception: Critical role of the prefrontal cortex. *Journal of Cognitive Neuroscience, 19*(6), 993–1003.

Sana, F., Weston, T., & Cepeda, N. J. (2013). Laptop multitasking hinders classroom learning for both users and nearby peers. *Computers & Education, 62,* 24–31.

Sandkühler, S., & Bhattacharya, J. (2008, January 23). Deconstructing insight: EEG correlates of insightful problem solving. *PLoS ONE, 3*(1), e1459.

Saunders, M. N. (1996, May). The physiology of boredom, depression and senile dementia. *Medical Hypotheses, 46*(5), 463–66.

Schreiber, L. A. (2004, April 21). Better brain surgery. *Discover Magazine.* Retrieved from http://discovermagazine.com/2004/apr/keith-black

Schultz, W., Dayan, P., & Montague, P. R. (1997, March 14). A neural substrate of prediction and reward. *Science, 275*(5306), 1593–99.

Schweighofer, N., Bertin, M., Shishida, K., Okamoto, Y., Tanaka, S. C., Yamawaki, S., & Doya, K. (2008, April 23). Low-serotonin levels increase delayed reward discounting in humans. *The Journal of Neuroscience, 28*(17), 4528–32.

Setzer, C. (1997). Excellent women: Female witness to the resurrection. *Journal of Biblical Literature, 116*(2), 259.

Sharot, T., Martino, B. D., & Dolan, R. J. (2009, March 5). How choice reveals and shapes expected hedonic outcome. *The Journal of Neuroscience, 29*(12), 3760–65.

Sharot, T., Riccardi, A. M., Raio, C. M., & Phelps, E. A. (2007, November 1). Neural mechanisms mediating optimism bias. *Nature, 450*(7166), 102–5.

Sherman, D. K., Mann, T., & Updegraff, J. A. (June, 2006). Approach/avoidance motivation, message framing, and health behavior: Understanding the congruency effect. *Motivation and Emotion, 30*(2), 165–69.

Shoda, Y., Mischel, W., & Peake, P. K. (1990). Predicting adolescent cognitive and self-regulatory competencies from preschool delay of gratification: Identifying diagnostic conditions. *Developmental Psychology, 26*(6), 978–86.

Shteynberg, G., & Galinsky, A. D. (2011). Implicit coordination: Sharing goals with similar others intensifies goal pursuit. *Journal of Experimental Social Psychology, 47*(6), 1291–94.

Siegel, D. J. (2010). *Mindsight: The new science of personal transformation* [Kindle version]. Retrieved from Amazon.com

Sio, U. N., & Ormerod, T. C. (2009, January). Does incubation enhance problem solving? A meta-analytic review. *Psychological Bulletin, 135*(1), 94–120.

Smither, J. W., & Walker, A. G. (2004, June). Are the characteristics of narrative comments related to improvement in multirater feedback ratings over time? *The Journal of Applied Psychology, 89*(3), 575–81.

Sousa, D. A. (2012). *BRAINWORK: The neuroscience behind how we lead others.* Bloomington, IN: Triple Nickel Press.

Steinberg, D. (2003, February 24). *Where is your heart? Some body part metaphors and euphemisms in biblical Hebrew.* Retrieved from http://www.adath-shalom.ca/body_metaphors_bib_hebrew.htm

Steinke, P. (2006). *How your church family works: Understanding congregations as emotional systems.* Herndon, VA: Alban Institute.

Stern, S. L., Dhanda, R., & Hazuda, H. P. (2009, October). Helplessness predicts the development of hypertension in older Mexican and European Americans. *Journal of Psychosomatic Research, 67*(4), 333–37.

Stiff, J. B., & Mongeau, P. A. (2002). *Persuasive communication* (2nd ed.). New York, NY: The Guilford Press.

Stone, L. (n.d.). *Continuous partial attention.* Retrieved from http://lindastone.net/qa/continuous-partial-attention/

Subramaniam, K., Kounios, J., Parrish, T. B., & Jung-Beeman, M. (2008, March). A brain mechanism for facilitation of insight by positive affect. *Journal of Cognitive Neuroscience, 21*(3), 415–32.

Tabibnia, G., Satpute, A. B., & Lieberman, M. D. (2008, April). The sunny side of fairness: Preference for fairness activates reward circuitry (and disregarding unfairness activates self-control circuitry). *Psychological Science, 19*(4), 339–47.

Takahashi, H., Kato, M., Matsuura, M., Mobbs, D., Suhara, T., & Okubo, Y. (2009, February 13). When your gain is my pain and your pain is my gain: Neural correlates of envy and schadenfreude. *Science, 323*(5916), 937–39.

Taylor, D. W., Berry, P. C., & Block, C. H. (1958). Does group participation when using brainstorming facilitate or inhibit creative thinking? *Administrative Science Quarterly, 3*(1), 23.

Thomas, W. H. (1996). *Life worth living: How someone you love can still enjoy life in a nursing home.* Acton, MA: VanderWyk & Burnham.

Thompson, L. (2009, August 24). *The health benefits of pet ownership.* Retrieved from http://www.elementsbehavioralhealth.com/behavioral-health-news/the-health-benefits-of-pet-ownership/

Vitello, P. (2012, August 1). George A. Miller, a pioneer in cognitive psychology, is dead at 92. *The New York Times.* Retrieved from http://www.nytimes.com/2012/08/02/us/george-a-miller-cognitive-psychology-pioneer-dies-at-92.html?pagewanted=all&_r=0

Waldman, D. A., Atwater, L. E., & Antonioni, D. (1998). Has 360 degree feedback gone amok? *The Academy of Management Executive, 12*(2), 86–94.

Walton, G. M., Cohen, G. L., Cwir, D., & Spencer, S. J. (2012, March). Mere belonging: The power of social connections. *Journal of Personality and Social Psychology, 102*(3), 513–32.

Waytz, A., & Mason, M. (2013, July). Your brain at work. *Harvard Business Review.* Retrieved from https://hbr.org/2013/07/your-brain-at-work/ar/1

Waytz, A., Zaki, J., & Mitchell, J. P. (2012, May 30). Response of dorsomedial prefrontal cortex predicts altruistic behavior. *Journal of Neuroscience, 32*(22), 7646–50.

Whalen, P. J., Shin, L. M., McInerney, S. C., Fischer, H., Wright, C. I., & Rauch, S. L. (2001, March). A functional MRI study of human amygdala responses to facial expressions of fear versus anger. *Emotion, 1*(1), 70–83.

Whiting, J., Jones, E., Rock, D., & Bendit, X. (2012, October). Lead change with the brain in mind. *Neuroleadership Journal, 4,* 1–15.

Wilson, T. D., & Gilbert, D. T. (2005, June). Affective forecasting: Knowing what to want. *Current Directions in Psychological Science, 14*(3), 131–34.

Wolpert, S. (2010, June 22). *Neuroscientists can predict your behavior better than you can.* Retrieved from http://newsroom.ucla.edu/releases/neuroscientists-can-predict-your-160549

Zaki, J., & Ochsner, K. N. (2012, May). The neuroscience of empathy: Progress, pitfalls and promise. *Nature Neuroscience, 15*(5), 675–80.

Zeidan, F., Johnson, S. K., Diamond, B. J., David, Z., & Goolkasian, P. (2010, June). Mindfulness meditation improves cognition: Evidence of brief mental training. *Consciousness and Cognition, 19*(2), 597–605.

CPSIA information can be obtained at www.ICGtesting.com
Printed in the USA
LVOW05s0028260315

432009LV00002B/2/P